POCKET
DICTIONARY *of*
BIBLICAL
STUDIES

ARTHUR G. PATZIA &
ANTHONY J. PETROTTA

InterVarsity Press
Downers Grove, Illinois
Leicester, England

InterVarsity Press, USA
P.O. Box 1400, Downers Grove, IL 60515-1426, USA
World Wide Web: www.ivpress.com
E-mail: mail@ivpress.com

Inter-Varsity Press, England
38 De Montfort Street, Leicester LE1 7GP, England
www.ivpbooks.com
ivp@uccf.org.uk

InterVarsity Press® is the book-publishing division of InterVarsity Christian Fellowship/USA®, a student movement active on campus at hundreds of universities, colleges and schools of nursing in the United States of America, and a member movement of the International Fellowship of Evangelical Students. For information about local and regional activities, write Public Relations Dept., InterVarsity Christian Fellowship/USA, 6400 Schroeder Rd., P.O. Box 7895, Madison, WI 53707-7895, or visit the IVCF website at <www.ivcf.org>.

InterVarsity Press, England, is the book-publishing division of the Universities and Colleges Christian Fellowship (formerly the Inter-Varsity Fellowship), a student movement linking Christian Unions in universities and colleges throughout the United Kingdom and the Republic of Ireland, and a member movement of the International Fellowship of Evangelical Students. For information about local and national activities write to UCCF, 38 De Montfort Street, Leicester LE1 7GP.

Cover illustration: Roberta Polfus

USA ISBN 0-8308-1467-1

UK ISBN 0-85111-268-4

Printed in the United States of America ∞

Library of Congress Cataloging-in-Publication Data

Patzia, Arthur G.

  Pocket dictionary of biblical studies/Arthur G. Patzia & Anthony J. Petrotta.

    p. cm.

  ISBN 0-8308-1467-1 (pbk.: alk. paper)

  1. Bible—Study and teaching—Dictionaries. I. Petrotta, Anthony J., 1950- II. Title.

  BR600.3.P38 2002

  220.3—dc21

                                                                      2001059399

British Library Cataloguing in Publication Data

A catalogue record for this book is available from the British Library.

P 19 18 17 16 15 14 13 12 11 10 9 8 7 6 5 4 3 2 1

Y 17 16 15 14 13 12 11 10 09 08 07 06 05 04 03 02

Preface

This volume of approximately five hundred entries conforms to the overall purpose of the InterVarsity Press pocket dictionary series by providing brief definitions of significant terms and key names that students encounter in introductory courses and beginning textbooks on the Old and New Testaments. We thank our students who, over our years of teaching, gave us blank stares, looked at us inquisitively or were bold enough to raise their hands for clarification when we as professors used terms that were familiar to our world of biblical studies but were foreign to them.

Our list of entries expanded and contracted over the months as we considered what terms were helpful to students engaged in biblical studies. Common biblical terms, names, places and other topics that one might find in a Bible dictionary were avoided since we wanted to focus mainly on terms having to do with the *study* of the Bible. On the other end of the scale, the more specialized vocabulary of various approaches to biblical studies or of Hebrew and Greek language and exegesis were avoided in favor of more general terms and concepts.

We focused on English terms, but in the field of biblical studies one necessarily comes across Hebrew-, Greek- and Latin-based terms, and we have included some of these. The list also includes several German words and phrases which have found their way into English texts and conversations as "loan" words. In cases where it was necessary or helpful to refer to the biblical languages, transliterations were provided for those who are studying the biblical languages or for those who want to pursue the terms further. Keeping the pocket dictionary to its limit also meant omitting most bibliographical references. Textbooks, dictionaries and other reference works will provide this information in abundance. The short list of abbreviations presents those that most commonly appear in textbooks and reference works, and is intended as an additional aid to students.

Cross-References
This pocket dictionary is cross-referenced using the following system:

☐ An asterisk (*) before a word or phrase indicates that an entry on that topic, similarly worded, appears elsewhere in the book.

☐ A *see*, followed by a subject and placed in parentheses, may be used instead of an asterisk to direct readers more clearly to a relevant entry.

☐ *See also* references at the end of entries direct readers to related topics.

☐ An alphabetized entry title with no definition is followed by *See* and the name of the entry under which the definition will be found.

Abbreviations
A list of abbreviations commonly encountered in biblical studies is included at the back of this book.

*   *   *

We are grateful to Dr. Daniel G. Reid, senior editor for reference and academic books at InterVarsity Press, for his vision in launching this pocket dictionary series, his guidance in selecting the contents of this volume, and his encouragement to complete the task. We hope that every reader will profit from the material

Arthur G. Patzia
Anthony J. Petrotta
Menlo Park, California

A

abomination of desolation. A phrase taken from the prophecy of Daniel (cf. Dan 11:31; 12:11) where the prophet states that the temple would be used for some future abominable and revolting act. Some scholars suggest that it refers to the time when Antiochus IV Epiphanes polluted the temple in 167 B.C. by sacrificing a pig on the altar (1 Macc 1:54); others claim that the reference is to the destruction of the temple in A.D. 70 (cf. Mt 24:15-16; Mk 13:14); some claim that the "abomination" is still unfulfilled but is predicted in 2 Thessalonians 2:3-4, where, in the coming rebellion, the "lawless one" will take over God's role in the temple—the ultimate act of sacrilege that marks the beginning of the end times.

acrostic. A poetic form where the initial letters of each line form a word, phrase, or alphabet. For example, Psalm 119 is structured around the twenty-two letters of the Hebrew alphabet (eight lines for each letter). Acrostics are sometimes thought to be mnemonic (memory) devices, but they are more readily viewed as literary or aesthetic devices whereby authors can use the constraints of the form (the acrostic itself) to contribute to the theme. In the case of Psalm 119, a *hymn in praise of *Torah, the author uses the twenty-two letters to show the total sufficiency of Torah.

agora. The central square of a Greek city, usually translated as the "marketplace." The square was surrounded by public buildings, temples, shops and so forth. Since many people would visit the agora for business, shopping, leisure and public assemblies, it served as an ideal location to proclaim the gospel (cf. Acts 16:19; 17:17).

agraphon. A Greek term (pl. *agrapha*) for an "unwritten saying" attributed to Jesus but not found in the canonical Gospels. Examples in the New Testament include Acts 20:35 ("remembering the words of the Lord Jesus, for he himself said, 'It is more blessed to give than to receive'"). Additional sayings include 1 Corinthians 11:24-25, the textual variant in Luke 6:5, some possible sayings included in certain apocryphal New Testament texts such as the *Gospel of Thomas* and *Gospel of Philip*, and some *papyrus fragments.

Akedah. *See* Aqedah.

Akkadian. Usually refers to the language of the Semitic people who inhabited lower *Mesopotamia where the city-state Akkad was located. Akkadian is also used generally of the Babylonian and Assyrian dialects. The language adopted the *cuneiform syllabic script. Eventually the Akkadian language replaced the older *Sumerian language, though Sumerian continued to be used in the scribal schools. Akkadian texts appear in the third millennium and continue into the first millennium B.C.

Albright, William Foxwell (1891-1971). American OT scholar and archaeologist. Albright used archaeological research to put the Bible on solid historical ground. In particular, he sought to show the essential reliability of the *patriarchs and the Mosaic traditions and laws. He was critical of *Wellhausen and *source criticism, and his critique found favor with many conservative scholars in America and elsewhere. He had an unparalleled knowledge of the languages and cultures of the ancient Near East. To many, Albright was known as the "dean of biblical archaeology."

Alexandrian school. An allegorical approach to interpreting the biblical text that, together with the *Antiochene school (literal approach), exerted great influence during the *patristic era (c. A.D. 100-750). The Alexandrian school, rooted in *Platonic philosophy and heir to the exegetical traditions of *Philo and *Origen, discovered symbols of divine truth in the lives and events portrayed in the Bible. This school also advocated a course of Christian action and theology that often went beyond the text itself. The adherents employed the *allegorical method of interpretation, which was an attempt to come to terms with a Christian use of the OT; their approach embraced the conviction that all Scripture is divinely inspired and, therefore, historical events teach divine truths, and intellectually offensive passages (e.g., passages with *anthropomorphic language and the like) are not to be taken literally. *See also sensus plenior.*

allegorical method. A method of interpreting a text in which the characters, events or places signify "deeper" meaning(s) than their literal meaning. The allegorical method was especially employed with difficult texts (e.g., the "sacrifice of Isaac" in Gen 22) or texts that no longer held the same power for later readers (e.g., for Christians, the temple or dietary laws were given new meaning in the light of the person and work of Jesus). These texts were given new life or wider significance, making them more accessible or more relevant for new contexts. The danger in the allegorical method is the violence done to the text in forcing correspondences that do not naturally correspond or cohere with the text. *See also* typology.

allegory. A literary form where a story is told for what it signifies rather than for its own sake. The characters and sometimes events or places are interpreted as abstract ideas or personifications of historical persons, which moves the focus from the personality of the character or the nature of the event itself. For example, in Nathan's story of the ewe lamb, the lamb itself is not the point of the story but rather is a personification of Bathsheba (2 Sam 12:1-14). Similarly, the vineyard in Isaiah's parable is Israel (Is 5:1-10). Some of the parables of Jesus also have obvious allegorical aspects (e.g., the parable of the sower, Mt 13 par. Mk 4 and Lk 8). Generally, in allegory the point is not so much that each item signifies something but that the allegory itself signifies a virtue, vice or type of character, or occasionally, a correlative historical person or event. *See also* metaphor.

alpha and omega. The first *(alpha)* and the last *(ōmega)* letters of the Greek alphabet. The phrase, "I am the Alpha and the Omega," is used for God (Rev 1:8; 21:6; see Is 44:6; 48:12) and for Jesus Christ (Rev 22:13; cf. also 1:17; 2:8). When attributed to Jesus, it designates him as the beginning (first) and ending (last) of everything, including designating him as the Creator, the fullness, and the climax of the universe (Rom 11:36; Eph 1:10).

ʿam hāʾāreṣ. A Hebrew phrase literally meaning "people of the land." Although there are references to the people of the land in the OT (Ezra 4:4; 10:2; Neh 10:30-31; Jer 1:18; 34:19; 37:2; 44:21), interpreters have given more attention to this group in *rabbinic literature, since it seems to illuminate a text like John 7:49: "But this crowd, which does not know the law—they are accursed." Most current scholarship questions the older view that the "people of the land" were regarded as impure sinners who were unworthy of salvation and were thus excluded from *synagogue worship.

amanuensis. A person, such as a scribe or secretary, hired to write from dictation or from a brief outline of a letter (from Latin *manu*, "hand"). Tertius is named the "writer" of Romans (16:22). Paul also employed other individuals, and he draws attention to the fact by commenting that he is closing the letter in his own hand (cf. 1 Cor 16:21; Gal 6:11; Col 4:18; 2 Thess 3:17). Silvanus is identified as Peter's amanuensis (1 Pet 5:12). This practice of using secretaries (see Jer 36:4) may account for some differences in style and language in some of the NT letters attributed to Paul and Peter.

Amarna tablets. *Cuneiform tablets consisting of mostly diplomatic letters, found at Tell el-Amarna on the Nile River. The tablets were discovered in 1887 by a woman digging in the mud for fertilizer. These texts, dated during the reign of Akhenaton (c. 1350-1334 B.C.), depict political and socioeconomic life in the ancient Near East, including Canaan and Syria, prior to the arrival of the Israelites from Egypt. Of primary interest for biblical scholars is the mention of the Apiru, a people living in Canaan in the Late Bronze Age (1550-1200 B.C.) and sometimes identified as the Hebrews. More likely they were outlaws or refugees of some type, since the word is used as a social rather than an ethnic designation.

Amenemope, Instruction of. *Didactic text of the Egyptian New Kingdom (c. 1567-1085 B.C.). This text extols the development of disciplined and modest behavior more than the development of political skills. Proverbs 22:17—23:11 is thought by many scholars to be dependent on the Egyptian proverbs of Amenemope. The style and language are remarkably similar, though the biblical proverbs are cast in the context of Israel's faith, not Egyptian teaching. For example, the proverb against robbing the poor or oppressing the afflicted is given a reason in Proverbs 22:23 ("for the LORD pleads their cause") that is absent from the Egyptian text. (A characteristic of biblical injunctions is the "motive clause," where a rationale is given as a means of instruction; *see also* Torah).

Amoraim. Designation of the *rabbinic teachers in both Palestine and Babylon during the third to sixth centuries A.D. (the Hebrew term means "speakers" or "interpreters"). These rabbis held the *Mishnah as authoritative for their own rulings and sought to elucidate the discussions therein. Their interpretations shifted the focus of Jewish thought from worship in the temple (which had been destroyed in A.D. 70) to worship in the *synagogue and home, with emphasis on prayer and morality, not the *cult.

amphictyony. A model used to explain the social organization of the tribes of Israel prior to the monarchy. This model, based primarily on the analogy of the ancient Greek sacral leagues, views Israel as a confederacy of twelve tribes organized around the *cult of Yahweh, their God, whose worship took place at a central shrine (e.g., first in Shechem, then in Shiloh). It is questionable that the amphictyony model adequately explains the social organization of Israel or is the clearest analogy. However, the biblical account of Israel's origins reflects that the tribes of Israel were organized around common religious institutions and beliefs.

aniconic. A term that means "without representation." It is used to describe the Israelite tradition, in which God was not represented by any images (cf. Ex 20:4).

anonymous. Literally, "nameless" (from the Gk *a*, "without," + *onoma*, "name"). A piece of literature that does not identify the author by name is considered anonymous. The four Gospels, for example, probably circulated anonymously for approximately fifty years before the current names of Matthew, Mark, Luke and John were attached to them. The book of Hebrews also circulated as an anonymous document before Paul's name was attached to it for a while. The historical books of the OT and many of the psalms do not have names attached to them. *See also* pseudonymity.

anthropomorphism. In the Bible and theology, a strategy of speaking of God in which human traits or emotions (the latter is known as "anthropopathism") are ascribed to God. For example, references to God's "right arm" or God "sitting" in the heavens and "laughing" are often said to be anthropomorphic and a reflection of "primitive" thinking about God. However, anthropomorphisms can be viewed as the language of immanence—God's nearness and relatedness to his creation. Thus, God's "walking" in the garden in the cool of the day (Gen 3:8) is less about putting a "human form" on God as it is a way of speaking about God's *involvement* in the world. In the case of anthropopathisms (e.g., God's laughter or anger), the depictions are not "irrational" ("emotional outbursts") but can be seen as part of God's response to human behavior and part of his will for creation. God, *in some sense*, may truly find some thought or action "funny" or a cause of "wrath" (cf. Ps 2:4-5). The difficulty of dealing with anthropomorphisms is illustrated by what we mean when we say that "God speaks" or that

"God hears." Are we saying that God has vocal cords and ears, or are we saying that such language reflects how God relates to people, where the give and take of speaking and listening characterizes the relationship? *See also* metaphor.

anthropopathism. *See* anthropomorphism.

antilegomena. According to *Eusebius, those books of the NT (Hebrews, 2 Peter, James, Jude, 1-3 John, Revelation) whose canonicity was disputed (Gk *anti*, "against," + *legō*, "say, speak") by the early church, as opposed to those books that were accepted (*homologoumena). *See also* canon.

antinomian. A term used to characterize believers in the early church who wrongly thought that salvation by faith in Jesus Christ freed them from all moral obligations and that they could sin with impunity (Gk *anti*, "against," + *nomos*, "law"). The problem of antinomianism is addressed in such NT passages as Romans 6:1-11 and 1 John (cf. 1 Jn 1:9-10). Some scholars link this attitude to early forms of *Gnosticism, where knowledge was placed above ethics.

Antiochene school. An approach to interpreting the biblical text that, together with the *Alexandrian school, exerted great influence during the *patristic era (c. A.D. 100-750). The Antiochene school built its *hermeneutic upon Aristotelian principles and was deeply influenced by the strong Jewish population in Antioch. In contrast to the *allegorical approach of the Alexandrian school, the Antiochenes employed what they termed *theōria* ("reflection, contemplation"), which for them meant a meaning of the text deeper than a mere historical approach, but still firmly rooted in the literal sense and historical context of ancient Israel. The Antiochene approach is closer to a modern understanding of *typology, since it made reference to the divine ordering of history (in contrast with the more symbolic approach of the allegorical method practiced in Alexandria). *See also sensus plenior*.

antitheses. In NT studies, the six contrasts between Moses' and Jesus' teaching presented in the Sermon on the Mount in Matthew 5:21-48. Each antithesis is introduced by the formula, "You have heard that it was said," followed by the antithetical response, "But I [Jesus] say to you."

antitype. *See* typology.

aphorism. A brief definition (Gk *aphorismos)*, statement, pithy saying or formulation of a truth. Biblical examples of aphorisms include "Train children in the right way, and when old, they will not stray" (Prov 22:6) and "For where your treasure is, there your heart will be also" (Mt 6:21). *See also* proverb.

apocalypse. Literally, an "unveiling" or "revelation." The term is employed in the opening words in the last book of the Bible, "The revelation *[apokalypsis]* of Jesus Christ" (Rev 1:1). It is also used by interpreters to describe certain "revelatory" parts of the book of Daniel, such passages as Isaiah 24—27 and Mark 13, and some noncanonical books. *See also* apocalyptic; apocalypticism.

apocalyptic. A term used to describe a literary *genre and worldview where "secrets" are revealed about the heavenly world or the kingdom of God (and the end of the world). These secrets are usually delivered through dreams or visions or by otherworldly messengers (e.g., angels) and are expressed in vivid symbols or metaphors. Apocalyptic works flourished during the Greco-Roman period (c. 200 B.C. to A.D. 200) and are not limited to biblical books but were part of the broader culture of the Mediterranean world. Often in apocalyptic literature an *admonition* is given to the audience to persevere and to be faithful. The community is warned that it will experience a time of suffering, but this will be followed by vindication of the righteous and a punishment of the wicked. *See also* apocalypse; apocalypticism.

apocalypticism. Usually used to describe a social group and especially the ideology or beliefs of those who adopt an *apocalyptic perspective. The origin of apocalyptic thought and the influences upon it are debated, ranging from prophecy to *mantic wisdom and *myth. Within the Jewish tradition, apocalyptic *eschatology stands in contrast with prophetic eschatology (where future events unfold from within human history, such as in Mic 4:1-4), with apocalyptic eschatology placing an emphasis on an "inbreaking" of God or his agents from outside the normal course of human events, often with an ending of the present world order and the resurrection of those who remain faithful. Apocalypticism testifies to God's rule over history, which gives the faithful a framework for action rather than passive acceptance or despair in a time of conflict and persecution. *See also* apocalypse; apocalyptic.

Apocrypha, the. The name given to a collection of books that were thought to contain "hidden" or "secret" truths (from the Gk *apokryptō*, "to hide, conceal"). The books of the Apocrypha are considered canonical by the Roman Catholic and Orthodox Churches but are not included in the Jewish or most Protestant Scriptures. The *apocryphal OT includes books that are still deemed important for Judaism and Protestant Christianity, such as 1 and 2 Maccabees and Wisdom of Solomon, even though they are not considered canonical. These books have a different status from the *apocryphal Gospels, letters and apocalyptic literature written between the second and sixth centuries A.D., and is not part of any Christian *canon. *See also* deuterocanonical books; Nag Hammadi Library; Oxyrhynchus papyri; gospel.

apocryphal. Generally used as an adjective to describe the *Apocrypha or any text or saying of doubtful authority or truthfulness. The story of the composition of the *Septuagint, as recorded in the *Letter of *Aristeas*, for example, is considered apocryphal.

apodictic law. A form of law characterized by personal address in the form of the imperative mood, "You shall not . . ." Usually no mitigating circumstances or details are given, and no consequences are specified, such as in Exodus 20:13: "You shall not murder." This is in contrast to *casuistic law.

apophthegm. A transliteration of the Greek, "to speak one's opinion freely" (pl. apophthegmata). In Gospel studies (particularly *form criticism), the term was used by Rudolf *Bultmann for Jesus' proverbial and wisdom sayings that were transmitted *orally but put into a historical context when they were written down by the Gospel authors (e.g., Mk 3:1-6; 7:1-23; 10:17-22; 12:13-17). Martin Dibelius used the term *paradigm* for the same type of material; Vincent Taylor used *"pronouncement story." *See also* chreia.

aporia. In *source criticism of the Gospels, a technical term indicating apparent abrupt transitions or structural inconsistencies that result when an author is attempting to incorporate material from different sources into a single document. Jesus' farewell discourse in John 14—16 is thought by some interpreters to contain several structural shifts of this kind.

apostolic parousia. The idea that even though Paul is not personally present in one of the churches, his apostolic authority is, nevertheless, present and should be felt either through the letter that he writes to the church (see Rom 1:8-15; 15:14-33; 1 Cor 4:14-21; 2 Cor 12:14—13:13; Philem 22) or through a designated envoy such as Timothy (1 Cor 4:17-20; Phil 2:19-24; 1 Thess 2:17—3:13).

apparatus, critical. The text-critical footnotes found on the pages of most editions of the Hebrew OT and Greek NT. These notes cite various manuscript sources and readings that either support or differ from the printed text. Current English versions of the Bible occasionally indicate important textual differences with the phrase "some ancient manuscripts omit" or "some ancient manuscripts add" in the footnotes. *See also* textual criticism.

Aqedah. A *rabbinic term referring to the story and the interpretations of Abraham "sacrificing" Isaac as told in Genesis 22 (*^{a}qêdâ* means "binding" [of Isaac]). In the biblical story God instructs Abraham to sacrifice his only son, Isaac, on Mt. Moriah as a test of Abraham's faith and perseverance. Abraham is obedient to this radical test, and the blessing on Abraham is reiterated not because of his obedience but as a reaffirmation of the promise and a recognition of the value of human obedience (Gen 22:15-18). The story is rich in tradition for Jews, Christians and Muslims, and is used for theological reflection on such diverse issues as obedience, martyrdom and God's providence.

Aquinas, Thomas (1225-1274). A medieval Italian theologian and Dominican monk whose systematization of theology in his *Summa Theologica* (a synthesis of Aristotelian philosophy and Christian faith) became the accepted and official teaching of the Roman Catholic Church. His biblical scholarship is also reflected in his sermons, expositions and commentaries on both the OT and NT.

Aramaism. Influences on the language, form and content of Greek texts from the Aramaic language. In the NT, Aramaic (or *Semitic) influences have been observed in the parables of Jesus and the interpretation (*midrash) of OT stories and concepts (e.g., Lk 24:21 picks up on the theme of "liberation" and recalls a midrash that identifies Moses as the one who would "set Israel free"). Aramaisms are particularly noticeable in the use of such terms as Abba, "father" (cf. Mk 14:36; Rom 8:15; Gal 4:6), and Tabitha, an Aramaic personal name (cf. Acts 9:36). *See also maranatha.*

aretalogy. A term describing the miracles, great deeds, supernatural powers, powerful acts and virtuous qualities of a god or a "divine man" (Gk *aretē*, "virtue"). In Gospel studies it refers to the miracles and miracle stories of Jesus recorded in the four Gospels. *See also* divine man.

Arianism. The beliefs of those who espouse the teachings of *Arius.

Aristeas, Letter of. A document purportedly describing the circumstances surrounding the translation of the OT into Greek. The author, Aristeas, probably a Jew living in Alexandria in the third century B.C., wrote a letter to his brother, Philocrates, telling of seventy-two delegates, six from each of the tribes of Israel, who were sent to Ptolemy II, king of Egypt, to translate the Law (*Torah) for his library. This library was to contain a worldwide collection of books. The task, according to the letter, was completed in seventy-two days, and all the translators agreed on the final translation. The story has many idealized elements, but the translation of the OT into Greek met many needs of the Greek-speaking Jews living in Alexandria. The translation, begun during the third century B.C., was not completed until the first century. *See also* apocryphal; Septuagint.

Arius (c. 256-336). An early church theologian from Alexandria, Egypt, who believed that Jesus, although fully human and the highest created being, was not fully divine because he did not share the same substance as God. Arius's beliefs (*Arianism) were declared heretical at the *Council of Nicea in A.D. 325.

Asherah. The name of the Canaanite mother goddess, the consort of the god El and the counterpart to the god Baal. In Babylon she was known as the "lady of voluptuousness" and elsewhere for her sexual appetite. Biblical references to Asherah usually pertain to wooden poles or trees associated with forbidden *cultic institutions (cf. Ex 34:13), especially cultic prostitution (cf. Hos 4:12-14). The prophetic indictment of worship of Asherah is a testimony to the lure of this practice throughout Israelite history.

Athanasius (c. 296-373). An early church theologian and apologist who was trained in the *catechetical school of Alexandria. Although he is known primarily for his opposition to the heretical doctrines of *Arius, he also developed several significant principles of biblical interpretation. As bishop of Alexandria, he devoted a large part of his thirty-ninth festal (festival) letter to his churches to announcing the date of Easter in A.D. 367 and listing the books of the OT and NT that he thought should be *canonical. His list of books was basically adopted by the Third *Council of Carthage in A.D. 397.

A.U.C. An abbreviation of the Latin *ab urbe condita*, or *anno urbis conditae* (literally, "from the city founding"), referring to the founding of the city of Rome. Dionysius, a Scythian monk, dated the beginning of the Christian era as it related to the founding of the city of Rome, which he dated at 754 B.C. Dionysius erred: it was 750 B.C. Thus we have the odd fact that the birth of Jesus is now dated to c. 4—6 B.C.

Augustine (354-430). Bishop of Hippo Regius in northern Africa (modern Bona in Algeria) from 395 to 430. In addition to such significant writings as his *Confessions, On Christian Doctrine* and *The City of God*, Augustine, along with *Athanasius, was instrumental in setting the limits of the biblical *canon that was adopted by the Third *Council of Carthage in 397. Because of his massive intellect, spiritual insight and exposition of Christian truth, he has been called "the greatest man who ever wrote Latin."

Augustinian Hypothesis. The opinion of *Augustine that the current canonical order of the Gospels (Matthew, Mark, Luke, John) is the actual chronological order in which they were composed.

autograph. The original manuscript or document of an author's work (from the Greek *autographos,* "written in one's own hand"). Since no autographs of any biblical book have been discovered, scholars must work with later copies.

B

Babylonian exile. The period of time from the destruction of the first temple (587 B.C.) and the deportation of King Zedekiah and others to the land of Babylon until the edict of Cyrus allowed the Jews to return to the land of Israel and rebuild the temple in 538 B.C. (cf. 2 Chron 36:22-23). The northern kingdom (Israel) had been conquered by the Assyrians and deported in 721 B.C. The prophets, Hosea and Amos in particular, had announced this destruction for the idolatrous practices of that kingdom. Micah and Isaiah, contemporaries of Hosea and Amos, said that the same fate would befall Judah, the southern kingdom, if it persisted in its ways. The Babylonian exile had a decisive effect on the theology of the Bible. The loss of the national symbols—land, temple, kingship—put into question Judah's identity as the people of God. The people's response to this crisis was to accept the prophetic indictment of their idolatry and to "return" in faith to the *covenant. Exile was seen as both punishment (for their sins, Lam 1:5) and promise (that God would not forsake his people, Lam 3:21-24). Many Jews remained in the new lands and did not return to the land of Israel. *See also* Diaspora.

Bar Kokhba. A Jewish zealot (his Hebrew name was Simon ben Kosiba) who led the second Jewish revolt (A.D. 132-135) against the Romans. Some scholars suggest that the assumed name Bar Kokhba (Aramaic, also spelled Bar Cochba), "son of the star," was a messianic title derived from Numbers 24:17, which states that "a star shall come out of Jacob, and a scepter shall rise out of Israel." In *rabbinic literature, a derogatory pun on his name portrayed him as Bar Koziba, "son of the lie," because of the defeat of his messianic aspirations.

Barth, Karl (1886-1968). Swiss theologian and father of neo-orthodoxy. Perhaps the most influential theologian of the twentieth century, Barth stressed the transcendence of God who, nonetheless, reveals himself in Jesus Christ. He trained under the liberal scholars of his day, but in his famous commentary on Romans, written while he was a pastor after the First World War, he broke with liberalism and sought to recover the reality of God's sovereignty as witnessed by the prophets and apostles. His massive *Church Dogmatics* contains many detailed and instructive examples of his *exegesis of Scripture.

Bat Qol. Hebrew, "daughter of the voice." The term is used by Jews to speak of the heavenly voice, but it is distinguished from prophecy, which is received by someone already in relation to God. A NT example of the Bat Qol is the divine voice heard at Jesus' baptism (Mt 3:17; Mk 1:11; Lk 3:22).

Baur, Ferdinand Christian (1792-1860). Professor of church history and dogmatics at the University of Tübingen, Germany, from 1826 to 1860. Baur developed a radical *historical-critical approach to the Bible that, among other things, questioned the supernatural accounts of the origins of Christianity, the unity of the canon and the apostolic authorship of most NT letters. He applied G. W. F. Hegel's philosophy (thesis—antithesis—synthesis) to early church history by proposing that the opposition between the Jewish Christianity of Peter (thesis) and the Gentile Christianity of Paul (antithesis) led to a reconciliation (synthesis) in the early catholic church of the second century A.D. *See also* Tübingen school.

B.C.E. "Before the Common Era." A term equivalent to the more traditional B.C. but without Christian or theological implications. The "common era" is the era "common" to or widely shared by Jews and Christians. This designation is more appropriate than B.C. in scholarship or conversations shared by Christians and Jews.

Bede, St. (c. 673-735). The "father of English history" and one of the most learned men of his time. When the Continent was entering the Dark Ages, the church in Northumbria, where Bede lived, benefited from the scholarship of Italy (brought by Theodore of Tarsus, the archbishop of Canterbury) and the devotion of the Celtic Church. Bede is known for his many writings and scholarship, including commentaries on many books of the Bible, such as the Gospels of Mark and Luke.

Benedictus. The traditional Latin name given to Zechariah's prophecy regarding John the Baptist (Lk 1:68-79). In Latin, the first sentence reads *Benedictus Dominus Deus Israel* ("Blessed be the Lord God of Israel"), but the prophecy continues as a *hymn of praise to God for his favor and *covenantal promises to his people, and a prediction of John's role as a prophet. *See also* Magnificat; Nunc Dimittis.

Bernard of Clairvaux (c. 1090-1153). Eloquent medieval preacher and founder of sixty-eight monasteries throughout Europe. As an interpreter, he is most famous for his sermons on the Song of Songs. These sermons reached a wide audience as Bernard drew upon the rich erotic imagery and related this experience to the personal, affective experience of God's love for us and our love for God. By way of *allegory, the *literal meaning was transferred to one's desire for (and union with) Christ.

biblical criticism. The application of rational judgments and methods for studying the biblical text with a view to sorting out the different stages of composition and the literary differences between and within the books. It is also used more generally to refer to the modern interpretation of biblical texts. Biblical criticism *as discriminating interpretation* has been practiced since communities first accepted these texts as authoritative; however, biblical criticism took a new turn in the eighteenth century with the study of the Bible as a "scientific" enterprise and not necessarily from a faith perspective. The methods and approaches have multiplied since its inception, but the underlying assumption remains that the Bible should be read as any other book would be read, using historical and literary methods to make judgments about a text's origin and meaning. One danger of biblical criticism lies in the potential loss of a distinctively theological reading of the text as the Word of God. *See also* Biblical Theology Movement; canonical criticism.

Biblical Theology Movement. Following the Second World War, a group of biblical scholars sought to find a unity within the Bible based upon the *underlying* assumptions and thought patterns of the text, even though the individual authors or books may express those patterns in different words or images. The movement accepted *biblical criticism and its results but wanted to recover the theological dimension in Scripture. God's revelation in history became the center point of much of the enterprise, although *salvation* history, more than any verifiable historical event, was the key to the text (the distinction was drawn more sharply by some than by others). Biblical theology for these scholars was a way to show the importance and lasting significance of the Bible for the Christian reader. Readers were encouraged to think "Hebraically" and were to focus on themes and concepts; they were to put themselves into the "world of the Bible" and its categories, not to think in abstract terms or "Greek" categories. The movement was roundly criticized at its central points, even from those within the movement (e.g., Brevard *Childs), and its influence waned. However, recent approaches to the study of the Bible, especially *canonical criticism, attempt to recover the need for a theological reading while avoiding the pitfalls of positing a "biblical mentality" or a thematic unity between the Testaments.

biblicism. A derogatory term describing an uncritical and unquestioning adherence to the Bible and one's literal interpretation of it.

bibliolatry. A pejorative term used to express an attitude of people who focus so much attention on the Bible *as a book to be venerated and idolized in itself* that they obscure more important issues about the Bible, such as its divine revelation from God transmitted through human authors.

binding of Isaac. *See* Aqedah.

binitarianism. A doctrine that denies the deity of the Holy Spirit by defining him as only an impersonal power of the Father and Son, who together share a single essence or substance. Initially, the doctrine was based on the close association of God the Father and Jesus the Son in such texts as Romans 4:24; 2 Corinthians 4:14; and 1 Timothy 2:5-6. As such, it differs from trinitarianism, which affirms the deity of three persons of the Godhead (Father, Son, Spirit). In discussions of early Christian worship, early Christian devotion to God the Father and the Son is sometimes described as binitarian or having a "binitarian shape."

Birkat Haminim. Literally, "the blessing of the heretics," but generally seen as a "curse" against Jewish Christians who were expelled from the *synagogue when tensions between Jewish believers and unbelievers increased (cf. Jn 9:22; 12:42; 16:2). The Eighteen Benedictions that were read in some synagogues include this phrase: "As for the apostates, let there be no hope, and in judgment cause the kingdom of arrogance soon to be destroyed. *Blessed are you, O Lord, who humbles the proud.*"

book of the covenant. *See* Covenant Code.

Book of the Twelve. A corpus of the twelve *Minor Prophets, consisting of Hosea, Joel, Amos, Obadiah, Jonah, Micah, Nahum, Habakkuk, Zephaniah, Haggai, Zechariah and Malachi. *See also* Nebiim.

Bornkamm, Günther (1905-1990). A German NT scholar who taught mainly at the University of Heidelberg, Germany. Although a student of Rudolf *Bultmann, he did not embrace his teacher's radical skepticism about the historical Jesus (cf. *Quest of the Historical Jesus). Bornkamm's significant monograph *Jesus of Nazareth* (ET 1960) sought to demonstrate the continuity between the Jesus of Nazareth as presented in the Gospels and the Christ of faith as believed and proclaimed in the church. He also was one of the first scholars to apply the principles of *redaction criticism to the Gospel of Matthew.

Bruce, Frederick Fyvie (1910-1991). A prolific and influential British evangelical scholar who spent most of his academic career at Manchester University in England. Although known mainly for his many commentaries on books of the NT, he also contributed to OT studies, biblical theology, NT history and the history of the canon.

Bultmann, Rudolf (1884-1976). A German NT scholar who had a distinguished teaching career at the University of Marburg (1921-1951). Bultmann was perhaps the most influential NT scholar of the twentieth century, and his studies, which reflect the influence of dialectical theology and existential philosophy, covered a wide range of issues, including *hermeneutics, the *historical Jesus, *form criticism, Johannine theology, Pauline theology, NT theology and the *history of religions school. *See also* apophthegm; demythologization; *Historie.*

C

canon. A term referring to the authoritative status of the final formation and collection of the biblical books (the term means "measuring rod, standard"). The order of these books sometimes differs (see *Tanak for the Hebrew order of the canon), and which books comprise the canon may differ (the Catholic canon contains the *Apocrypha, which are sometimes referred to as "deuterocanonical"), but the list of books in the canon are sanctioned as the norm from which doctrine and practice are derived. The Jewish canon was discussed at *Jamnia/Yavneh after the first Jewish War (A.D. 66-74), though disputes continued into the second century. The list of the twenty-seven books in the NT canon was given authoritative status by *Athanasius, bishop of Alexandria, in the fourth century. *Canon* thus refers to the books themselves or their authoritative function in the community of believers and testifies to both the adaptability and stability of Scripture. *Canonization* refers to the process by which these writings became recognized as uniquely authoritative. *See also* Council of Carthage; deuterocanonical books.

canonical criticism. An approach that seeks to interpret the biblical books with respect to their authoritative status and theological context within the Bible. Canonical criticism thus focuses on the final form of the biblical texts rather than their earlier stages of composition or transmission (though recognition of the stages plays an integral role in some uses of this approach). Furthermore, canonical critics argue that the object of biblical interpretation is theological reflection within a community of faith. For example, *Torah and the Gospels have a special function in the canon. They are set apart as first and foundational; hence the *Prophets in the OT and Paul in the NT should be read in the light of the Torah and the Gospels respectively, even though the Prophets and Paul's letters may predate the present form of the Torah and Gospels. Canonical criticism sees the Bible as "Scripture," as authoritative writings of the community of faith, and incorporates theological reflection as part of the reading of a text. *See also* Childs, Brevard.

Captivity Epistles. A term used for the letters of Paul that are thought to have been written during his imprisonment (primarily at Rome, but some would argue for Caesarea and Ephesus as well; also called Prison Epistles). For many scholars these letters include Ephesians, Philippians, Colossians, Philemon, 1 and 2 Timothy, and Titus.

Carthage, Council of. *See* Council of Carthage.

casuistic law. A form of law characterized by an "if . . . then" condition where an action and its consequences are stipulated, and mitigating circumstances or considerations are specified. A biblical example is Exodus 21:12-13: "Whoever strikes a person mortally shall be put to death. If it was not premeditated, but came about by an act of God, then I will appoint for you a place to which the killer may flee." It stands in contrast to *apodictic law.

catalogue of vices and virtues. The listing of vices and virtues by NT writers. This device, which is found in Stoic philosophy, was adapted and utilized by various NT writers in the context of ethical instruction. Often the terms *Lasterkatalog* (vice list) and *Tugendkatalog* (virtue list) occur in biblical studies as loanwords from the German. The NT contains extensive lists or catalogues of vices (e.g., Rom 1:29-31; Gal 5:19-21; Eph 5:3-5) and virtues (e.g., 2 Cor 6:6-7; Gal 5:22-26; Phil 4:8).

catechesis, catechetical. The moral and religious material in *oral or written form for instructing believers in matters of faith and ethics within the context of a religious community (from the Gk *katēcheō*, to "inform, instruct, or teach"). Sections of Deuteronomy, the Gospels (especially Matthew) and the epistolary literature were originally used for this purpose. *See also* paraenesis.

Catholic Epistles. A designation for seven NT letters (James, 1 and 2 Peter, Jude, 1, 2, and 3 John) because, unlike Paul's epistles, they were not addressed to a specific church but to Christians in general (*catholic* generically means "general" or "universal"). Thus, for example, James wrote to "the twelve tribes in the Dispersion" (1:1), and 1 Peter is addressed to "the exiles of the Dispersion" (1:1) throughout various Roman provinces. Hebrews is not included because it is addressed to a particular audience, even though we cannot identify that audience with certainty.

C.E. "Common Era" (i.e., common to Christians and Jews). This abbreviation is often preferred in scholarship and conversations shared by Jews and Christians instead of the more common and Christian-derived A.D. See also *B.C.E.

charisma. A term taken from the Greek *charis* ("gift, grace") and used in the NT to describe various spiritual gifts (*charismata*) that are present in the church, such as tongues, prophecy, wisdom, knowledge and faith (cf. Rom 12:6-8; 1 Cor 12:8-10, 28; 1 Pet 4:10-11).

charismatic. A person who possesses and manifests any of the spiritual gifts (*see* charisma). However, in current popular usage it usually describes a person with the gift of *glossolalia, or "tongues." It is also used of a person with a charming and powerful personality, one who is able to inspire the allegiance of others. In the OT the "spirit of the Lord" upon certain individuals enabled them to prophesy (see Judg 3:10; Num 11:25, 29; Is 42:1; 62:1-2; Joel 2:28-29; Zech 12:10).

chiasm. Derived from the Greek letter *chi* (which is shaped like a letter X), a rhetorical device whereby parallel lines of a text correspond in an X pattern, such as A-B-C-B'-A' (in this case the center of the chiasm is C, and on either side line A will correspond to line A' and so forth). For example, a chiastic pattern (without a C element) may be observed in Mark 2:27 and set out in the following fashion:

A: The sabbath was made
   B: for humankind,
   B': and not humankind
A': for the sabbath

The pattern can be as simple as a verse in Mark or as elaborate as a whole poem, a parable or a book. In using this device, an author can show both progression of thought and intensification of meaning. Chiasm is a way of "layering" words and themes.

Childs, Brevard S. (1923-). American OT scholar. Childs is best known for his critique of the *Biblical Theology Movement, of which he was a part, and his advocacy of *canonical criticism, although he eschews the terms as a methodology. Childs's concern is to render a coherent interpretation of the biblical text as sacred Scripture for both the church and the *synagogue. It is the "shape" of the canonical text—its scope and purpose—that guides one's interpretation, not a methodology or a particular theory of the prehistory of the text.

chreia. A technical term (pl. chreiai) used in ancient Greek rhetoric for pithy phrases or short sayings (*epigrams) and actions told about or in honor of an important person and useful for daily living (hence the Gk *chreia*, something "needful, necessary, lacking"). A number of scholars believe that the early church adapted certain sayings and actions of Jesus to the chreia form (cf. Mk 1:14-15; Lk 3:10-11; 19:45-46; Jn 4:43-44).

christological titles. Various titles attributed to Jesus of Nazareth in the NT, titles such as Christ, Lord, Son of God, Son of Man, Messiah, Savior and Servant. These titles serve as a way of defining Christ's nature and mission; however, a full understanding of NT christology must take into account other factors as well.

Christophany. The appearance or manifestation of Christ to his disciples, such as after the resurrection (Mt 28:1-10, 16-17; Mk 16:9-14; Lk 24:13-49), at the transfiguration (Mt 17:1-8; Mk 9:2-8; Lk 9:28-36) and the Lord's appearance to Paul on the Damascus road (Acts 9:3-16).

Chronicler. The author(s) of the book of Chronicles (and perhaps Ezra and Nehemiah). Chronicles, written after the *Babylonian exile, dramatizes the history of Israel from Adam through the end of the monarchy; Ezra and Nehemiah describe the events surrounding the return to the land and the rebuilding of the temple. The Chronicler has a deep concern for the monarchy and temple, and interprets blessings and punishment as retributive justice for the actions of the kings. In these books, speeches and prayers of the kings and prophets are employed in an almost sermonic fashion, which contributes to the overall structure of the book. The Chronicler cajoles and inspires his readers to follow *Torah, especially as it is centered on worship in the temple.

Chrysostom, John (c. 354-407). Bishop of Constantinople noted for his excellent preaching (Gk *chrysostomos* means "golden-mouthed"). Chrysostom belonged to the *Antiochene school and was perhaps the most distinguished of the *patristic preachers. His *exegesis is found in a series of sermons he delivered largely in the cathedral in Antioch. These sermons are characterized by spiritual and moral application of the literal sense of Scripture. Chrysostom often announced his lesson for the next service and encouraged his congregation to read the lessons so they would have a better understanding of his sermon.

Clement of Alexandria (c. 155-220). The first Christian scholar of note in the *patristic era (c. A.D. 100-750). Clement was installed as the head of the *catechetical school of Alexandria in 190, where he wrote most of his works. Noted more for his theological writings, he nevertheless wrote a commentary on Scripture in the mode of the *Alexandrian school. He is also noted as the teacher of *Origen.

codex. The "book" form (as opposed to a scroll) of an ancient manuscript of either papyrus or vellum. The codex was first used by the Romans for business and legal transactions but was also utilized by the early church as they collected and bound NT manuscripts together.

coherence, criterion of. One of the criteria used by NT scholars to determine the authenticity of certain sayings of Jesus. Sayings are considered authentic if they "cohere" or "agree" in form and content with material established by other principles such as the criteria of *dissimilarity and *multiple attestation. *See also* criteria of authenticity.

Comma Johanneum. A textual variant in 1 John that should be excluded from the text (Gk *komma,* "a piece, that which is cut off"). The disputed textual variant occurs in 1 John 5:7-8 ("There are three that testify *in heaven, the Father, the Word, and the Holy Spirit, and these three are one. And there are three that testify on earth"*) and was inserted by Erasmus into his Greek text. It was subsequently included in the King James Version. The words in italics above are not authentic and should be "cut off," that is, not be included in the NT.

Community Rule. *See also Rule of the Community.*

comparative midrash. *See* inner-biblical exegesis.

complaint psalms. *See* lament psalms.

composite. A text made up from different sources or texts. In the NT, 2 Corinthians and Philippians are sometimes described as composite texts because some scholars believe that they incorporate more than one source (in this case letters) into the final text.

composition criticism. A technical term taken from the German *Kompositionsgeschichte*, which, like *redaction criticism, emphasizes the creative, theological and literary role of the Evangelists in their composition of the four *Gospels.

conflict story. A brief narrative in the Gospels that records a pronouncement of Jesus in the context of conflict with someone, usually one or more religious authorities, such as a scribe or Pharisee (cf. Mt 12:1-8; 21:23-27; 23:1-39). A closely related term is *controversy dialogue*, such as in Jesus' confrontation with Satan during his temptation (Mt 4:1-11 and par.).

Constantine (c. 288-337). The first Christian Roman emperor. Constantine sought to unite the church and expand its influence. In 330 he established Constantinople as his capital on the site of the Greek city Byzantium.

Conzelmann, Hans (1915-1989). A German NT scholar. Conzelmann is often associated with Gunther *Bornkamm and Ernst *Käsemann as the "post-Bultmannians" who broke with their teacher Rudolf *Bultmann on a number of issues, particularly on the credibility of the historical Jesus as presented in the Gospels (see *Quest of the Historical Jesus). Through his pioneering work in *redaction criticism, Conzelmann produced his most famous book, *Die Mitte der Zeit* (1954, literally "the middle of time," unfortunately translated into English as *The Theology of St. Luke*, 1960). Here Conzelmann claims that Luke replaced Mark's *eschatology of the imminent return of the Son of Man with a more settled perspective of a history of the church set forth in his two-volume work *Luke-Acts.

corporate personality. The idea that in ancient Israel the identity of an individual was bound up in the community. Thus an individual person could stand for a group as, for example, in the Psalms, where an individual "I" (often a king, David) stands for the nation of Israel. Some scholars, such as William Robertson Smith, tied this notion to a theory of Hebrew psychology in which a person's individuality merged almost fluidly with the group. His theory is now largely discredited, but revised notions of corporate personality continue to play a role in biblical studies, since it is broadly recognized that in the cultures of the Bible the community was regarded as at least as important as the individual.

corpus. A "body" (Latin *corpus* means "body"; pl. *corpora*) or collection of writings of a specific kind. Thus, within the NT, we speak of the Pauline corpus and the Johannine corpus as literature attributed to Paul and John. Its use may vary among contemporary scholars. For example, those who question the authorship of certain letters attributed to Paul may refer to a Pauline and a *deutero-Pauline corpus.

Council of Carthage. The Third Council of Carthage in A.D. 397, which was probably the first church council to have officially endorsed the twenty-seven books that constitute the NT *canon.

Council of Jamnia. *See* Jamnia, Council of.

Council of Jerusalem. The meeting of early church leaders such as James, Peter, Paul, and various apostles and elders in Jerusalem around A.D. 49 (Acts 15:1-35). This was a crucial gathering in the development of the early church because it legitimized Paul and Barnabas's mission to the Gentiles. In doing so, the council recognized that Gentiles could become believers without adhering to Mosaic laws, although it exhorted Gentiles "to abstain only from things polluted by idols and from fornication and from whatever has been strangled and from blood" (Acts 15:20; see Gal 2:1-14; *Noahic covenant).

Council of Nicea. An ecumenical council convened by the emperor Constantine in A.D. 325 to deal with the Arian controversy. *See also* Arius; Arianism.

Council of Trent. A theological council (1545-1563) of the Roman Catholic Church organized to respond to the theological challenges that emerged from the Protestant Reformation. In addition to discussing many theological issues, the council also made several pronouncements on the biblical text, its interpretation and the canon of Scripture. The council accepted the OT canon acknowledged by Jews and Protestants, but it also included a number of books from the *Apocrypha as well.

covenant. The Bible's most widely used *analogy* for the relationship between God and his people (other analogies include parent-child, shepherd-flock). The covenant (Heb *bᵉrît*, Gk *diathēkē*) relationship, as conceived in the OT, is a bilateral relationship in which God offers the children of Israel a special status among the nations of the earth. He will be their God, bestowing an identity and blessings upon them, and they will be his people, obeying the stipulations of the covenant (the *Torah). Mention is often made of the asymmetrical nature of the covenant—that is, God as sovereign and the people as vassals. However, the mutuality of the covenant is most often portrayed, each party having obligations and responsibilities (surrounding the blessings and obedience). The OT portrays numerous covenants (with Noah, Abraham, Moses, David, the new covenant), but these are never enumerated; rather, they build upon each other and fill out what is meant by the analogy of the covenant relationship. The OT prophets especially looked forward to the new covenant, which would extend and enhance what was already inherent in this relationship that God had with his people (cf. Jer 31). *See also* suzerainty treaties.

Covenant Code. A designation by modern scholars for the law code found in the text of Exodus 21—23 (also called the "book of the covenant"). The term is sometimes used of the document found in the temple by King Josiah that resulted in his reforms (see 2 Kings 22; 2 Chron 34).

covenant renewal. A purported celebration of an annual (New Year's) renewal of Israel's *covenant with Yahweh, guaranteeing peace and prosperity to his people. Some scholars (e.g., Sigmund *Mowinckel) make this suggestion on the basis of the so-called *enthronement psalms (Ps 93; 97; 99) and the common ancient Near Eastern New Year celebrations that were associated with the enthronement of the king or, as in *Ugarit, the dying and rising of the god Baal.

credo, creed. A formal or confessional statement of faith usually drawn from the *cultic/religious life of believing communities (Latin *credo,* "I believe"). In the OT, creedal summaries revolve around such themes as the exodus, the conquest of the promised land, the *covenant at Sinai, and the like (see, e.g., Deut 6:1-11, 20-24; 20:5-9; Josh 24:2b-13; 1 Sam 12:8; Ps 78; 105; 135; 136). Deuteronomy 26:5 ("A wandering Aramean was my ancestor; he went down into Egypt and lived there as an alien, few in number, and there he became a great nation, mighty and populous") is thought to be the oldest creed in the OT. In the NT, creedal statements appear as fixed formulas in several places, as for example, in 1 Corinthians 15:3-5 ("For I handed on to you as of first importance what I in turn had received: that Christ died for our sins in accordance with the scriptures, and that he was buried, and that he was raised on the third day in accordance with the scriptures, and that he appeared to Cephas, then to the twelve"; see also Phil 2:5-11 and 1 Tim 3:16).

criteria of authenticity. A general term referring to the various tests NT scholars use to determine the historical authenticity of the sayings of Jesus in the Gospels. *See also* coherence, criterion of; dissimilarity, criterion of; multiple attestation, criterion of.

crux interpretum. An essential or puzzling passage that requires a resolution and becomes a central point of an argument (the term is Latin for "cross" or "torment" of interpretation). For example, Jesus said, "From the days of John the Baptist until now the kingdom of heaven has suffered violence, and the violent take it by force" (Mt 11:12). This and other passages have long presented problems for translators and interpreters and can have a bearing on how we understand the kingdom of God.

Cullmann, Oscar (1902-1999). A German NT scholar. Cullmann taught at the University of Strasbourg and is mainly remembered and appreciated for his insistence that Jesus Christ must be understood in light of God's entire history of salvation (cf. *Heilsgeschichte)*—a concept developed in his *Christ and Time* (ET 1952) and *Salvation in History* (ET 1967). His christology (*Christology of the New Testament;* ET 1959) is described as a "functional christology" because Cullmann focused more on the work of Christ than on Christ's nature and being.

cult, cultus. A term used for public worship in general, especially the festivals, rituals and sacrifices in service to God or the gods. Popular usage employs the term as a derogatory designation for new religious movements, but scholars employ it as a descriptive term for worship of any kind. For example, the distinction between clean and unclean animals in the *Pentateuch was a cultic distinction, a daily reminder to observant Jews to be "holy"; the dietary laws were reminders of holiness and practices of holiness, and they prepared one to worship the Lord even in mundane matters of daily meals and to separate oneself from profane practices that led away from worship.

cuneiform. A style of writing in which a clay or wax tablet was inscribed by a reed instrument, resulting in patterns of "wedges" (Latin *cuneus*) representing symbols and syllables. This method of writing was a standard form throughout the ancient Mediterranean world beginning in 3100 B.C. Even though the alphabet form of writing emerged in approximately 1700 B.C., cuneiform continued into the first century B.C. Much of the history and tradition of the ancient Near East is preserved in cuneiform texts. *See also* hieroglyph.

Cynic. A philosophical movement founded by Diogenes of Sinope (c. 400-325 B.C.) that was more of a way of life (lifestyle) than a school of philosophical principles. Diogenes was given the name "Diogenes the Dog" ("cynic" derives from the Gk *kyōn*, "dog") because of his shameless behavior in public. Cynics lived "according to nature," emphasizing the simplicity and frugality of life rather than its luxuries.

Cyril of Alexandria (375-444). Patriarch of Alexandria and outstanding exegete of the *Alexandrian school. Cyril firmly adhered to the *allegorical method but, because of his contact with *Jerome and the *Antiochene school, also concerned himself with the literal sense of the biblical text. For Cyril, however, the literal sense derived its meaning from the thing signified and not simply the words themselves. Thus for Cyril the spiritual sense was often the "literal" meaning of a passage because everything in a text could have meaning beyond the simple meaning of a term. For example, according to Cyril, when the prophet Micah says "This [one?] is [our] peace" (Mic 5:5), he is referring to Christ himself and not simply the peace effected by Christ.

Cyrus. Leader of the combined armies of Persia and Media who conquered Babylon in 539 B.C. Babylon was experiencing a period of instability when Nabonidus, its last monarch and a supporter of the moon-god Sin, was opposed by the priests of Marduk, Babylon's chief deity. Cyrus took advantage of this rupture and "entered Babylon without a battle," perhaps aided by the priests who welcomed him in the name of Marduk and wrote a glowing inscription of his victory. Cyrus declared peace for all, issuing an edict for the Jews in exile to return to their land and rebuild the temple (2 Chron 36:22-23). Isaiah calls Cyrus the Lord's "shepherd" (44:28) and his "anointed" (45:1). *See also* Babylonian exile; Diaspora.

D

Damascus Document. Three documents (portions of Sirach, an Aramaic portion of the *Testament of Levi* and the *Damascus Document*) found in the *genizah (storage closet) of an old synagogue in Cairo in 1896 and published in 1910 under the title of *Fragments of a Zadokite Work.* The most prominent of these documents is called the *Damascus Document* because Damascus is mentioned several times, but it is also referred to as Cairo Damascus (CD) because it was discovered in Cairo. Copies of this document were also found at *Qumran and are designated as QD. The document contains an admonition and a series of laws, and it mentions the Teacher of Righteousness, who is believed to have been a founding figure of the *Essene community of Qumran.

Dead Sea Scrolls. The collection of approximately 850 Jewish manuscripts (mostly fragmentary) discovered by shepherds in 1947 in caves near the shore of the Dead Sea. These scrolls represent all the biblical texts except Esther, as well as many nonbiblical texts, including commentaries and paraphrases of biblical books, and liturgical and *eschatological works. The scrolls have assisted scholars in establishing the text of the Hebrew Bible as it was centuries before the Masoretic Text, which was previously the earliest available manuscript (see *Masoretes; *textual criticism). Equally important, the scrolls have shed light on early Judaism and early Christianity by unveiling the thought and practice of one group among the diversity of perspectives that existed within Judaism at that time. The communities that preserved these texts were ascetic with respect to laws of purity and eschatological with respect to history and God's rule. *See also* Essenes; Qumran.

Decalogue. The brief, largely negative prohibitions (literally, "ten words," *deka logoi*, but commonly known as the Ten Commandments) found in Exodus 20:1-17 and (with slight variations) in Deuteronomy 5:6-21 that serve as a summation of *Torah. The Decalogue has greatly influenced Western philosophy and ethical thought, but its purpose was to give the people of God an identity in the *covenant relationship that God established on Mt. Sinai following the exodus from Egypt. Their special character can be seen in several ways, notably, that these words are given directly to the people of God without mediation from Moses, unlike other laws in the *Pentateuch. Moreover, they have a special name: the term *Decalogue* derives from the Hebrew designation found in Exodus 34:28 (*ᵃśeret haddᵉbārîm*, "ten words/things"). The characteristic feature of the Decalogue, the brief, negative prohibitions ("You shall not . . . "), points to its special nature as well, with the personal address and no punishment specified for violation. The numbering of the Ten Commandments varies within different faith communities. The Decalogue is portrayed as a gift from God and an expression of God's will, not an abstract ethical code. *See also* apodictic law; casuistic law.

deconstruction. An approach to the text that is not so much a method as it is a recognition or a philosophy of how texts work. Usually texts are thought to have a clear meaning, but in deconstruction their stated purpose is undermined, since the point of view of the text is hidden. For example, in the opening chapters of Job, the doctrine of "retributive justice" (*see lex talionis)* seems assumed by everyone: Job is a righteous person and is duly blessed by this righteousness. In the poems that follow, the doctrine is questioned if not actually rejected. Finally, in the epilogue, Job is restored, which seems to undermine all the questioning of the doctrine in the poems. Some would argue that the book "deconstructs" the doctrine and then deconstructs its own deconstruction. Deconstruction is closely associated with postmodern thought, which emphasizes plurality and diversity in texts and in worldviews.

demiurge. A subordinate or inferior deity who is believed to be responsible for creating the material world. In *Philo the term is often used in his discussion of creation, but only to contrast the Creator God *(ktistēs)* with a mere "craftsman" *(dēmiourgos)*. In *gnostic thought the term refers to an inferior and ignorant being who is creator of the material world but who is less than a supreme god (cf. *Marcion).

demythologization. A technical term (German *Entmythologisierung)* generally associated with the hermeneutics of Rudolf *Bultmann. Bultmann's method was to strip away ancient mythical elements from the text, such as angels, demons, a three-storied universe, the virgin birth, resurrection, and the like, as objective realities and to interpret mythical language existentially, that is, asking what these myths say about human existence.

derash. The homiletical exposition of Scripture in *rabbinic Judaism (the Hebrew root means to "search out," hence "exposition"). The rabbis developed rules and techniques for arriving at nonliteral uses of a biblical text for purposes of ethical or practical application. The term is used in contrast to **peshat,* the "plain" meaning of a text. *See also* midrash.

deuterocanonical books. Books that are not included in the Hebrew canon but are found in the Greek Old Testament (LXX; *Septuagint). These books are more commonly called the *Apocrypha, and to one extent or another are part of the Catholic or Orthodox canons of Scripture. The Protestant Reformers, following Martin *Luther, accepted only those books that were found in the Hebrew canon, but the Roman Catholic *Council of Trent in 1546 declared the *Apocrypha (with the exclusion of 1 and 2 Esdras, Prayer of Manasseh, and 3 and 4 Maccabees) to be canonical. Thus the adjective deuterocanonical, which means literally "second-canon," can be viewed as pejorative by Christian communions that include these books in their canon of Scripture.

Deutero-Isaiah. *See* Second Isaiah; Isaiah, multiple authorship of.

Deuteronomist. According to the *Documentary Hypothesis, the author(s) of the D source in the *Pentateuch. The D source is essentially made up of Deuteronomy, though its perspective may be found in Joshua, Judges and the books of Samuel and Kings. This source is thought to preserve traditions that circulated in the northern kingdom, probably in prophetic circles, before the fall of Samaria in 721 B.C., but were not written until the *Babylonian exile. The so-called D source employs a highly rhetorical style, verbose and *paraenetic, exhorting the people of God to purity in worship and loving obedience to God in the *covenant relationship. *See also* Deuteronomistic History; Documentary Hypothesis.

Deuteronomistic History. A designation for the work of the author(s) responsible for Deuteronomy and the history of Israel as told in Joshua, Judges, Samuel and Kings (the Former *Prophets). Martin *Noth argued that the similarity of language and themes in these books points to an individual hand rather than multiple authors (as in *source criticism, which posits several authors, or the traditional view that Samuel and Jeremiah authored Joshua through Kings). Scholars who follow this view now usually talk about a "Deuteronomic school" rather than a single author, but the unity and theological perspective are still adhered to. According to this view, the Deuteronomistic Historian interpreted the history of Israel through the lens of obedience or disobedience to the *covenant as spelled out in Deuteronomy and selected his material according to these principles. *See also* Documentary Hypothesis.

deutero-Pauline. Literally, a "deutero" ("second") Paul. The term is used in NT studies for epistles attributed to Paul but whose authorship is questioned because of certain linguistic, theological and historical factors (e.g., 2 Thess, Col, Eph, 1 and 2 Tim, Tit). *See also* Pseudepigrapha; pseudonymity.

Diaspora. Reference to Jews living outside the land of Israel in places such as Egypt, Asia Minor and Mesopotamia, usually through enforcement by a conquering nation, such as in the *Babylonian exile. (Jews will often use the term *gālût,* which means "captivity, exile.") In fact, the history of the Jews in Diaspora is longer than the history of the Jews living in a Jewish state in Palestine. The Egyptian enslavement of the Israelites is the *paradigm for Jewish exile and the hope that God will gather his people again (Deut 30:3-5).

Diatessaron. An early continuous narrative of the life of Christ based on the four Gospels, composed around A.D. 170 by Tatian (c. A.D. 120-173), a Syrian Christian apologist. The name *Diatessaron* is derived from the Greek *dia tessarōn,* "through the four [Gospels]."

The *Diatessaron* was used extensively in the Syrian churches for several centuries until it was finally ordered to be replaced by the fourfold Gospel collection.

diatribe. In antiquity, a form of rhetoric identified by short ethical discourses, rhetorical questions and dialogues, and argumentative speech, in which the author or speaker debates with an imaginary person (interlocutor) in order to instruct the audience. Although initially utilized by such philosophical schools as the *Stoics and *Cynics, some of its characteristics are reflected in the NT (cf. Rom 6:1-4; 12—15; Gal 5—6; Eph 4—6).

didache. A term referring to the teaching (Gk *didachē)* or instruction of the early church, as distinguished from its preaching (Gk *kērygma).*

Didache, **the.** An *anonymous manual of church instruction (also known as *The Teaching of the Twelve Apostles),* believed to have been written sometime between A.D. 85-150, possibly in ancient Syria. It is a unique collection of early Christian sayings and liturgical instructions on worship, baptism, the Eucharist and church leadership. Its three divisions include a section on the "two ways" (1.1—6.2), a manual of church order (6.3—15.4) and an *apocalyptic closing (16.1-8).

didactic. An adjective used of verses or texts that seek to instruct (cf. *didache),* often with moral intent, or to influence conduct. Many *proverbs are designated didactic sayings by *form critics. Proverbs 19:17 is one such example: "Whoever is kind to the poor lends to the LORD, and will be repaid in full."

dirge. *See* lament psalms.

discourse analysis. The study of the structure of coherent units of text that have a discernible context. Discourse analysis focuses on how language is used in a text and includes the subdisciplines of text-linguistics, which examines textual cohesion and the development of argument, and pragmatics, which studies the interaction between speech and the shared presuppositions that remain unarticulated. In pursuit of these goals, discourse analysis may draw on the fields of *rhetoric, anthropology, sociology, semiotics, *literary criticism and *reader-response criticism.

dissimilarity, criterion of. A criterion of authenticity in which sayings of Jesus are judged to be authentic if they are "dissimilar"—

that is, distinct or unique from sayings or beliefs common to the early church or ancient Judaism. *See also* coherence, criterion of; criteria of authenticity; multiple attestation, criterion of.

dittography. An unintentional duplication of a letter, word, phrase or sentence when copying a manuscript. For example, the *Masoretic Text of 2 Kings 7:13 repeats a whole clause, "since those left here will suffer the fate of the whole multitude of Israel," while the *Septuagint and other early texts and translations omit the second occurrence. In some Greek NT manuscripts duplication is found in such passages as Mark 12:27; Acts 19:34; and 1 Thessalonians 2:7. *See also* haplography; homoioteleuton.

divine man. A person or spiritual leader endowed with miraculous powers manifested through miracles, healing, exorcisms, and the like. In the ancient Mediterranean world, a Neopythagorean philosopher named Apollonius of Tyana (d. c. A.D. 98), epitomized this type of person, called a *theios anēr*. Later exaggerations of his virtuous life and manner were often used by anti-Christians in comparing him to Jesus. When NT scholars refer to a "divine man christology," they usually focus on the miraculous powers of Jesus' person and ministry. *See also* aretalogy.

docetism. An early Christian heresy emerging in the first century that denied the full humanity of Jesus and thus the reality of his sufferings and death. In other words, Jesus just "seemed" (Gk *dokeō*, "to seem, suppose") to be God fully incarnate. A good example of an attempt to combat this heresy is 1 John (e.g., 1:1-4; 4:1-3).

Documentary Hypothesis. A theory about the origins and composition of the *Pentateuch. This hypothesis arose during the eighteenth century as a result of new methods for studying the texts (cf. *source criticism). The Documentary Hypothesis posits that, rather than Moses authoring the Pentateuch, it went through a process of composition over several centuries, in which various sources were compiled into the final text. Questioning Mosaic authorship was not new, since even in the Middle Ages the great Jewish commentator *Ibn Ezra challenged the idea that Moses was the sole author of the Pentateuch. In the eighteenth century, the new methodology (measuring and mastering knowledge by empirical means) provided the analytical tools for a sustained critique of the single-author hypotheses. It was not until the nineteenth century that Julius *Wellhausen, building on the work of K. H. Graf, drew together not only literary analysis but a historical scheme to explain the sources, a *Religionsgeschichtliche* approach. The key ingredient in the historical reconstruction was the supposition that the prophets were the religious innovators of monotheism and that the priests with their *cultic practices came after the prophets and their ethical demands. Wellhausen identified four sources in their historical order: *Jahwist (J), *Elohist (E), *Deuteronomist (D) and *Priestly (P). These sources are commonly referred to as JEDP. Recently the hegemony of the Documentary Hypothesis has eroded as more scholars find unifying plots and themes in the stories of the Pentateuch. Most scholars still use the Documentary Hypothesis as their starting point for discussion, but attention has turned to the nature of Hebrew narrative and how words and themes link stories and concerns. *See also* literary criticism.

Dodd, C. H. (1884-1973). British NT scholar. Dodd has often been called the leading British NT scholar of the mid-twentieth century. His legacy includes work on the parables, early Christian preaching and the Fourth Gospel. *The Interpretation of the Fourth Gospel* (1953) is regarded as his greatest book. However, his emphasis on *realized eschatology in Jesus' words and deeds has been criticized because it fails to account for the future dimension in NT *eschatology.

dominical saying. Derived from the Latin *Dominus* (Lord), a reference to any saying attributed to Jesus, such as "I am the light of the world" (Jn 9:5).

double tradition. In Gospel studies, a reference to the fact that similar saying of Jesus appear twice in the Gospels—once in a setting located in Mark's Gospel, and a second time in settings found in Matthew and Luke. This supposedly demonstrates that Matthew and Luke used a second source for their sayings of Jesus (*Q).

doxology. In the NT, a form of praise, blessing or glory to God (Gk *doxa*, "praise, glory," + *legō*, "to speak") used in the context of worship and often ending with an "Amen." Philippians 4:20 offers one example: "To our God and Father be glory forever and ever. Amen" (cf. Rom 1:25; 16:27; Eph 3:21; 1 Tim 1:17; Rev 1:6; 7:12).

Driver, S. R. (1846-1914). British Hebrew and OT scholar. Driver mediated German critical scholarship to a wider English-speaking audience. He won respect through his moderation, lucid arguments and reverent treatment of the Bible. He is best known for his work on the *Hebrew and English Lexicon of the Old Testament* and his commentaries on Genesis, Deuteronomy and Job.

DtrH. Abbreviation for *Deuteronomistic History.

E

early catholicism. A technical term in NT studies based on the hypothesis that the early church developed from a rather loosely organized *charismatic community under the direction of the Holy Spirit in the apostolic age to a rather formal or "institutionalized" community in the postapostolic age, especially in such areas as church order, doctrine, leadership, and the sacraments. The *Pastoral Epistles are usually proposed as examples of this later development. *See also Frühkatholizismus.*

Ebionites, Ebionism. A Jewish-Christian sect that is first mentioned in the writings of *Irenaeus, a second-century church father. Both the Greek *Ebionaioi* and Latin *Ebionaei* are transliterations of the Hebrew and Aramaic word for "the poor." It appears that this group settled east of the Jordan, adopted an ascetic mode of life, and emphasized full observance of the Mosaic law, thus reducing the significance of the person and work of Christ.

Ebla. An ancient city whose remains were found at Tell Mardikh, south of Aleppo, in Syria. Excavations of the tell (mound) began in 1964, and eventually over four thousand texts were found. Though not mentioned in the Bible, this city was large and important in the ancient Near East, being inhabited from the third millennium B.C. until the first millennium A.D. Initially, scholars thought that the texts found at Ebla had a direct relevance to biblical studies (claims were made of references to Sodom and Gomorrah and biblical names), but most scholars now espouse the more modest appraisal that these texts increase our general knowledge of *Semitic languages and the cultural heritage of Israel's neighbors (specifically the Syrian culture c. 2400-1600 B.C.) rather than offering direct references to biblical characters or practices.

Eichhorn, Johann Gottfried (1752-1827). Father of modern "introductions" to the Bible. Eichhorn lectured on the OT, NT, *Semitic languages, and literature and culture in relation to world history. While accepting the notion of divine revelation in Scripture, he nonetheless reserved the right to interpret that revelation through modern knowledge. He applied the new *historical criticism to the Bible, tracing the development of the literature historically rather than following the traditional order of the *canon.

Eichrodt, Walther (1890-1978). German OT scholar who sought to reestablish the legitimacy of OT theology. Eichrodt combined literary and historical-critical research with systematic principles to obtain a comprehensive and coherent picture of OT faith. Eichrodt argued that the unity of OT beliefs (which had eroded under the questions raised by *historical criticism) is found in the idea of *covenant. His *Old Testament Theology,* which he structured in three parts—God and People, God and World, God and Man—is considered one of the most influential theologies to emerge from the *Biblical Theology Movement. *See also* Rad, Gerhard von.

eisegesis. Reading meaning *into* a text rather than reading a meaning *from* a text (*exegesis).

ekklēsia. A Greek term usually translated as "church," "gathering," "assembly," or "congregation." Outside of Scripture it could stand for any group that assembles; in the *Septuagint it occasionally refers to the *qāhāl* of Israel (the people of Israel assembled to hear the word of God). In the NT it became a standard term for the church.

Elohist. According to the *Documentary Hypothesis, the author(s) of the E source in the *Pentateuch who prefers the word *Elohim* when referring to God. The existence of a separate and continuous E source has increasingly been viewed as problematic, and source critics today are often inclined to eliminate it or speak of E as an editorial layer. But in the classical formulation of the Documentary Hypothesis, the so-called E source is thought to have been written in the northern kingdom of Israel, perhaps as early as the ninth century. Its emphasis on sites such as Bethel, its use of "Horeb" for Mt. Sinai and its parallels between Moses and Elijah suggest this provenance. The stories reflected in E begin with Abraham's call and conclude with the death of Moses. Theologically, *covenant stands at the center of the Elohist's perspective, and obedience to covenant is paramount. One is to "fear" God, which entails both awe and obedience. For the Elohist, all the people would be prophets like Abraham, Jacob, Joseph and Moses: "Would that all the LORD's people were prophets, and that the LORD would put his spirit upon them" (Num 11:29).

emendation. A correction made to a manuscript based on text-critical considerations. Emendations are usually made when there is a superior reading from either another manuscript or an earlier translation. An example of an emendation would be the correction of an obvious scribal mistake (*dittography; *haplography, etc.) or a textual solution for a particularly difficult text that seemingly makes little or no sense without some kind of emendation. This latter correction is called a "conjectural" emendation because there is no textual support for it; rather it rests on the judgment of scholar(s). *See also* textual criticism.

encomium. Enthusiastic praise or eulogy (Gk *enkōmion*). Originally, such poetic phrases were used by Pindar, a Greek lyric poet (c. 518-c. 438 B.C.), to celebrate athletic and military victories.

Enoch, **books of.** *Pseudepigraphal books attributed to Enoch (see Gen 5:21-24), largely *apocalyptic in nature. The extant books of *Enoch* are known today as *1 Enoch, 2 Enoch* and *3 Enoch.* Although a few Greek and Aramaic fragments of *1 Enoch* exist, the only complete manuscript of it is preserved in Ethiopic, which was regarded as sacred Scripture in Ethiopia (*2 Enoch* is preserved in Slavonic, *3 Enoch* in Hebrew). A reference in Jude 7 to material found in *1 Enoch* indicates that the literature was known—and perhaps even regarded as authoritative—by some Christians in the first century. Later, however, the literature was rejected by the church, and most copies of it were lost.

enthronement psalms. Psalms that speak of the exaltation or enthronement of the Lord. An example of an enthronement theme is seen in Psalm 97:9: "For you, O LORD, are most high over all the earth; you are exalted far above all gods." The enthronement psalms (47; 93; 96—99) share two characteristics: they call the nations and creation to praise *Yahweh, and they give a reason for the praise (something the Lord has done or some attribute of his). *See also* covenant renewal; hymn.

Enuma Elish. A Babylonian creation text that tells how the god Marduk killed the goddess Tiamat and then created the world from her dismembered parts. Hermann *Gunkel argued that the biblical story of creation in Genesis is dependent upon this tale, especially since the order of created things in the two stories is remarkably similar. However, recent scholarship shies away from arguing for dependence; the differences between the two stories are as striking as the similarities. Fragments of *Enuma Elish* were found in the mid-nineteenth century, and the story could date as far back as the second millennium B.C.

epic. A term used by literary critics for long narrative poems that treat great or serious subjects. These poems are written in an elevated style and center on a heroic (often quasi-divine) figure upon whose actions the fate of a nation depends. The term is extended by some scholars to refer more modestly to works that exhibit the epic "spirit" in their treatment of an important subject. In this latter sense, the book of Job may be classified as an epic, but on the whole the domestic realism of biblical stories and the role of the Lord in the affairs of creation resist the classic epic form. *See also* literary criticism.

epigram. *See* proverb.

epigraphy. The study and interpretation of ancient inscriptions such as the *Moabite Stone.

epiphany. A divine disclosure (Gk *epiphaneia*, "to appear, manifest") to humanity. In the OT, for example, God "appears" to Adam and Eve (Gen 1—3), Abraham (Gen 17:1), Moses (Ex 3), and so on. In the NT, *epiphany* refers to various occasions when Jesus appeared to humanity (Lk 1:78-79; Jn 1:1-18; 2 Tim 1:10; Tit 2:11-14) and will appear again at his return (2 Thess 2:8; 1 Tim 6:14). The Christian church celebrates the Feast of Epiphany on January 6 (twelve days after Christmas), commemorating Jesus' manifestation to the Gentiles through the visit of the magi (Mt 2). *See* Christophany.

episcopacy. An ecclesiastical system in Christianity governed by bishops (Gk *episkopeō*, "to oversee, take care of"). NT references to bishops indicate leaders who provide care and oversight in the church (Phil 1:1; 1 Tim 3:2-7; Tit 1:7-9;1 Pet 2:25).

eponym. A term used of a person whose name represents the characteristics of a group, usually the descendants of that person (Gk *epi* + *onoma*, "name upon"). In Genesis 12—50 the *patriarchs are sometimes claimed to be *eponymous* since, for example, Esau is explicitly identified as Edom, and the sons of Jacob are all identified with the tribes of Israel ("Israel," which means, "one who strives with God," is itself a name change after Jacob wrestles with God; see Gen 32:22-32).

Erasmus, Desiderius (c. 1466-1536). A Dutch biblical and *patristic scholar, philologist and *textual critic. Erasmus translated, edited and interpreted a large number of Greek and Latin manuscripts during his lifetime. He is credited with editing the first critical edition of the Greek NT in 1516 in Basel, Switzerland, a text that was revised several times in succeeding years. The translators of the King James Version of 1611 relied heavily on the Greek text of Erasmus and other editions produced from his work. *See also* Textus Receptus.

eschatology. A Greek-derived term that means the study of (or belief about) the last times (Gk *eschatos*, "last [things]"). Eschatological language and thought are pervasive in the OT and NT, and in *Second Temple Judaism and early Christian literature. In the OT we find eschatological thought especially in the *Prophets, with their use of the phrases "day of the Lord" or "in that day." For Israel's prophets, that day would be a time of judgment by God for the disobedience of Israel (Amos 5:18-20). However, the prophets also saw a time of restoration from the judgment when a *remnant would return to the land of Israel in faithful obedience to God (Hos 14:1-7). The restoration would inaugurate a time of peace when the law of the Lord would instruct all peoples (Mic 4:1-4). NT eschatology picks up on these images and, by combining them with *apocalyptic thought, extends them to speak of the time when God will bring about the end of the old age and the beginning of the new, when even death itself will have no power and God will dwell in the midst of creation (Rev 21:1-5). *See also* parousia; realized eschatology.

Essenes. One of the sects of Jews (along with the Pharisees and Sadducees, among others) that existed in Palestine during the NT period. For reasons that remain unclear, the Essenes are not mentioned specifically in the NT, but *Josephus describes them in his works. With the discovery of the *Dead Sea Scrolls in 1947, scholars renewed their interest in the group, since one of the scrolls was the *Rule of the Community, which detailed the practices of the community at *Qumran. The precise relationship between the Qumran (Dead Sea) community and the Essenes is still open to conjecture (Josephus mentions two groups of Essenes, one that married and one that did not). From the fragments of knowledge that we can piece together, it seems that the Essenes viewed themselves as the true Israel who adhered strictly to the *covenant made with God. Some may have separated themselves entirely from any outsiders (even other Jews), though they may have participated in temple worship on a limited basis.

etiology. A story (*saga) that tells the origin of a place name, a tribe or a ritual. For example, the creation of the woman in Genesis 2 is seen as an etiology of marriage: "Therefore a man leaves his father and his mother and clings to his wife, and they become one flesh" (Gen 2:24). The story of Jacob naming the place where he had his dream of a ladder reaching to heaven and of God reiterating the promise of Abraham (Gen 28:10-22) may be seen as an etiology for the place name Bethel ("house of God"), which was formerly called Luz (Gen 28:19). *See* legend.

Eucharist. Another term for the Lord's Supper. It is taken from the Greek verb *eucharisteō* ("to give thanks"), referring to the prayer of thanksgiving offered for the body and blood of Christ (see 1 Cor 11:23-26). The earliest references to the sacrament as Eucharist are in *Didache 9.1, *Ignatius (*Phld.* 4) and *Justin Martyr (*Apol.* 1.66).

Eusebius (c. 260-340). Bishop of Caesarea, commonly referred to as "the father of church history" because of the writing of his *Ecclesiastical History*. This history consists of ten books, and covers events and Christian doctrine of the church from the apostolic age to the time of *Constantine. Eusebius's work enters into biblical studies for various reasons, most frequently for evidence he gives of what Christians of the first centuries thought about the authorship and *canonicity of the NT books.

exaltation of Christ. A term synonymous with the resurrection and ascension of Christ. Luke, for example, uses either resurrection, ascension or exaltation as a sequel to the cross. Elsewhere in the NT, exaltation affirms that Jesus Christ is enthroned as the Lord of glory in the heavenlies with God (Eph 1:20; 2:6; Phil 2:9; Heb 7:26).

execration texts. Curses on enemies inscribed on pottery and then shattered. In Egypt, archaeologists found broken bowls (and other material) dating mostly to the Middle Kingdom (c. 2100-1800 B.C.) on which the names of Egyptian enemies were written. A curse ("execration") was exacted on these enemies by writing their names on the bowls and then smashing them. The names found on some of the fragments indicate that Egypt had interaction with, or control over, Canaan during this period (mention is made of Askelon, Ekron, Hazor and Jerusalem).

exegesis. To interpret a passage on its own terms (Gk *exēgeomai*, "to lead, draw out"). It usually refers more specifically to a verse-by-verse or phrase-by-phrase explanation. The goal in exegesis is to analyze passages carefully so that the words and intent of the passage are as clear as possible. Speculation is not prized, but attention to word meaning, form, structure, context (historical and biblical) and theology is usually addressed. Exegesis tends to be descriptive more than prescriptive; however, many readers engage in exegesis of the Bible for the ultimate purpose of finding guidance on spiritual matters, and thus relevance becomes part of the task of interpreting a passage. *See also* eisegesis; hermeneutics.

exile. *See* Babylonian exile; Diaspora.

exodus. The deliverance of the Israelites from slavery in Egypt into a new land (see Ex 3:1-12). Historically reconstructing the movement of God's people into and out of Egypt is difficult because references to the Israelites are lacking in Egyptian records. However, this is the defining event of God's dealing with the Israelites and continues to be a source of theological significance for Jews and Christians.

F

farewell discourse. A technical term describing a genre in biblical and extrabiblical literature that features a farewell speech by someone about to die (often including instructions and warnings) to a group of family members, friends or disciples. Such speeches were given by Jacob (Gen 48—49), Moses (Deut 31—34) and

Joshua (Josh 23—24). The *Testaments of the Twelve Patriarchs* is a notable example in the OT *pseudepigraphal literature. Examples in the NT include Jesus' farewell discourses to his disciples (Jn 13—17) and Paul's farewell to the Ephesian elders (Acts 20:17-38). The German word *Abschiedsrede* ("farewell address") is often retained in English translations of German originals.

feminist hermeneutics, feminist criticism. Approaches to interpretation that begins less with the biblical text and more with the concerns of feminism as a worldview. It recognizes that women have been marginalized by men throughout history. That is, women have not had access to positions of authority and therefore have not had adequate influence on social structures and roles. Feminist criticism adopts different approaches to the text, but the major strategy is to expose the means by which women have been written out of texts and the underlying justification by those texts. Feminist biblical critics range from those who seek out and expose the many ways women are suppressed in the Bible (even when a women is named, she frequently has little or no voice to speak; e.g., the stories of Sarah being passed off by Abraham as his sister) to those who find that even in a male-dominated text "pro-women" elements can be found and utilized. A feminist approach, then, not only seeks to understand what is being said about women in the text, but also evaluates the texts in the light of feminist concerns.

Fertile Crescent. The land from the Tigris and Euphrates Rivers on the Persian Gulf through Palestine to the Mediterranean Sea and down to the Nile River in Egypt. Egyptologist J. H. Breasted coined the term in 1917 because this area forms an arc or crescent-shaped landmass. The Tigris, Euphrates and Nile Rivers are the source of its fertility, providing water for agriculture and associated commodities (wool, hides, linens, etc.). Consequently, the lands became densely populated and trade flourished. The Fertile Crescent also became a place of many battles as kingdoms fought for control of the trade routes or independence from oppressive practices of the dynasties that developed. The history of the Bible unfolds against this social, economic and political backdrop in which Israel is the landmass through which Egyptian and Mesopotamian kingdoms passed.

fertility cult. Worship of gods who promised bountiful harvests in response to the sacrifices of their adherents. Agriculture was of central importance to ancient Near Eastern life, and productivity of the land was often tied to religious beliefs and *cultic practices. For OT studies, the *Ugaritic texts that center on the god Baal symbolize the link between the fertility of the land and plentiful rainfall. The story of Elijah and the prophets of Baal (1 Kings 18) reflects the influence of this thinking on Israel and the prophetic opposition to it.

Festschrift. A collection of scholarly essays published to commemorate or honor a significant scholar, usually issued on the occasion of the person's birthday or retirement from an academic career. The German term is a combination of two words, *Fest* (celebration) and *Schrift* (writing).

form criticism. An interpretive approach that seeks to uncover the *oral tradition that is embedded in the written texts we now possess and to classify them into certain categories or "forms" (German *Formgeschichte*, "history of forms"). These literary forms (*laments, *hymns, etc.) are thought to have had a particular function in the *Sitz im Leben* ("setting in life") in which they originated. For example, Psalm 24 has the form of an entrance liturgy and may have originated with a ceremony in which the ark was brought into the temple, or with a yearly festival in which the *enthronement of the Lord was celebrated. The psalm, however, works equally well with any symbolic entrance into a worship setting (e.g., Handel's use of this psalm in his oratorio, the *Messiah*). In NT studies, form-critical scholars such as Martin Dibelius, Rudolf *Bultmann and Vincent Taylor classified Jesus' sayings into categories such as *paradigms, *legends, *parables, *miracle stories and *pronouncement stories. Form criticism is helpful in identifying the different forms of literature (*see* genre) and the typical elements of those forms (thus highlighting the different ways authors use those forms), but it is more speculative and less successful in establishing the life setting of the forms. *See also* Fragment Hypothesis; *Gattung;* oral tradition.

Former Prophets. *See* Nebiim.

Formgeschichte. *See* form criticism.

formulas, pre-Pauline. Expressions, phrases, confessions, *creeds, *hymnic material and the like that are found throughout Paul's letters but inherited from the early church. Paul himself writes that he received *(paralambanō)* a body of tradition and then passed it on *(paradidomi)* to his congregations personally and in his letters (e.g., Rom 1:3-5; 4:24-25; 10:9-8; Phil 2:5-11; 1 Tim 3:16 *paradosis*).

Four-Document Hypothesis. *See* Four-Source Hypothesis.

Four-Source Hypothesis. Also known as the *Four-Document Hypothesis, the theory that the *Synoptic Gospels are based on four discrete sources. In the study of the sources that the Evangelists used to compose their Gospels, B. H. Streeter expanded upon the *Two-Source Hypothesis and proposed that, in addition to Mark and *Q, there were *M and *L sources as well. M and L represent material that is unique to Matthew and Luke respectively.

Fourth Philosophy. The name ascribed by *Josephus to a "sect of Jewish philosophy." Josephus, in the context of describing the three prominent Jewish "sects"—Pharisees, Sadducees and Essenes—speaks of a "fourth philosophy" that originated with Judas the Galilean (*Ant.* 18.1.6 §§23-25). Some scholars think that he uses Fourth Philosophy to refer to the Zealots. Others suggest that it probably refers to a group of Pharisees who advocated resistance to foreign rule and oppression through obedience to the *Torah rather than through armed rebellion.

Fragment Hypothesis. A theory used in the context of discussing the formation of biblical documents such as the *Pentateuch and the *Gospels. For the Pentateuch, this is an alternative theory to the *Documentary Hypothesis and maintains that rather than the Pentateuch being composed from a few documents (J, E, D, P), each of which were continuous literary works with a certain perspective, it was composed from numerous and varied fragments of written tradition. For the Gospels, scholars suggest that the disciples and other followers of Jesus remembered a significant amount of Jesus' words and deeds. But before these early eyewitnesses died, it was necessary to hear these stories from them again. These "fragments" may have been collected and categorized according to their content and form. *See also* form criticism; oral tradition.

Frühkatholizismus. *See* early catholicism.

G

Gattung. A conventional textual pattern (made up of smaller identifiable units called *forms)* that may be classified with others of its type. The German term *Gattung* is used of these general classifications or genres (e.g., *saga, *legend, *Gospel), while a smaller conventional unit is called *Form* (e.g., *hymn, *miracle story, *pronouncement story, *woe oracle). A related term, *Gattungsgeschichte,* refers to the historical study of these classifications or genres. Thus *Gattungsgeschichte* ("genre history") is to be distinguished from *Formgeschichte,* in which one focuses on smaller literary units that were originally *oral in nature. *See also* form criticism; genre; genre criticism.

gehenna. The "valley of Hinnom" (Heb *gê hinnōm;* Gk *geenna;* Latin *gehenna),* a ravine southwest of Jerusalem that connects with the Kidron Valley, as well as an image of destruction of the wicked. In the OT we learn that it was a place where children were sacrificed and burned to the god Molech (2 Kings 23:10; 2 Chron 28:3; 33:6), but it was also a site where dead animals and garbage were burned. In the NT *geenna* it is a graphic image of the punishment and destruction of the wicked (Mt 5:22; 10:28; 23:33; Mk 9:43-47; cf. Is 66:24) and thus is frequently translated into English as "hell."

Gemarah. *See* Talmud.

genizah. A chamber or storage closet in ancient synagogues for keeping old and unused copies of sacred texts. *See Damascus Document.*

genre. A term used by literary critics to refer to literary species or forms (from the French word for "style"). Subject matter, structure and style are taken into account when identifying a genre. NT authors employ *Gospel, letter and *apocalypse, among other genres. *See also* genre criticism.

genre criticism. An approach to the text that seeks to classify literature into forms or species. Classifications of genres are numerous and varied, ranging from tragedy and comedy to lyric and satire. The criteria for classification are variable, and care must be taken in classifying biblical genres, since no theoretical works on poetics exist from the biblical period, explaining how the various literary forms were employed. Furthermore, mere classification is not necessarily helpful unless some comment on the significance of the classification is included. Nevertheless, establishing a passage's genre can aid one's understanding or help one to avoid misreading Scripture. For example, an understanding of Psalm 51 as an instance of the *lament genre might help a reader not to focus too narrowly on the biographical elements in the superscription. In an effort to connect the words of the psalm with the events of David's life, a reader might miss the obvious lament and penitential nature of the psalm and lose the emotive call to repentance that the psalm is seeking to move the reader to accept. Genre criticism seeks to classify passages or texts according to form, style and content; it assumes that this classification is crucial to understanding the text.

Geonim. *Rabbinic teachers in Babylon during the mid-sixth to the mid-eleventh centuries A.D. *Diaspora Jews looked to them to settle issues of faith and practice. They established the Babylonian *Talmud as the standard text over the Palestinian *Talmud.

Geschichte. See Historie.

Gilgamesh Epic. Stories surrounding a famous *Mesopotamian king, Gilgamesh, who lived during the third millennium B.C. The stories deal with the destiny of humankind, with life and death, and other matters, but it is their recounting of a flood that has captured the attention of most biblical scholars and sparked many debates about the uniqueness of the biblical story. The stories of Gilgamesh went through various revisions and have been found throughout the ancient Near East (including Megiddo in Israel). Scholars are generally more cautious these days in positing links with the stories of the Bible, but these extrabiblical stories add to one's understanding of the cultural milieu of the Bible and thus can aid in understanding words, forms, customs and concerns.

gloss. A name given to words, phrases or verses that first appeared as clarifications or corrections in the margins of a text but then were added or incorporated secondarily into the text itself. For example, the clarification that a scribe placed into the margin at John 5:3-4, regarding the stirring of the water at the pool of Beth-zatha, was eventually brought into the text in several manuscripts (see NRSV footnotes).

glossolalia. The phenomenon of ecstatic speech (from the Gk *glōssa,* "tongue," + *laleō,* "to speak") that first occurs on the day of Pentecost (Acts 2:1-13) and then on subsequent occasions in the early church (cf. Acts 10:44-46; 19:6). The apostle Paul refers to speaking in "various kinds of tongues" as one of the spiritual gifts (1 Cor 12:10, 28) and as a legitimate manifestation of prophetic inspiration in the worship service at Corinth (1 Cor 12—14). Questions continue among scholars whether this is a special language of angels, some foreign unknown language or a dialect of a known language (Acts 2:6). Some ecclesiastical traditions believe that this phenomenon ceased with the apostolic age and should not be desired or practiced today, while others believe in its contemporary manifestation and encourage those who have the gift to practice it.

gnosis. A Greek noun meaning "knowledge" (verb *ginōskō*, "to know"). *See also* gnostic; Gnosticism.

gnostic. An adherent to *Gnosticism, or someone who places an unusual amount of value on esoteric spiritual knowledge.

Gnosticism. In a broad sense, a complex religious and philosophical movement that flourished between the first century B.C. and the fourth century A.D., which claimed that a true understanding of God, the self and salvation comes through special revelation and knowledge. Since there is no single gnostic system as such, there is no unanimous agreement among scholars on its definition and teaching. But when speaking of the first century, it is common to refer to Gnosticism as an early Christian heresy that stressed privately revealed knowledge above that which is generally available to everyone through the Scriptures. Since Gnosticism did not become a significant movement until after the NT era, it has become common in NT studies to speak of a protognosticism or incipient Gnosticism within first-century Christianity.

gospel. A term taken from the Greek *euangelion* ("good news") and thus a reference to the Christian message. Mark begins his story of Jesus as "The beginning of the good news [*archē tou euangeliou*] of Jesus Christ" (Mk 1:1), and soon it, and the accounts of Jesus by Matthew, Luke and John, were referred to as *a* or *the* Gospel(s). The Four Gospels as we now know them were *anonymous—that is, they were probably circulated for approximately fifty years before the specific names of Matthew, Mark, Luke and John were attached to them.

Gospels, canonical. The four Gospels that circulated throughout the churches in the Mediterranean world, then were collected and finally canonized by the church at the Third *Council of Carthage in A.D. 397 (as opposed to *apocryphal gospels).

Gospels, Synoptic. *See* Synoptic Gospels.

Graf-Wellhausen Hypothesis. *See* Documentary Hypothesis.

Griesbach, Johann Jakob (1745-1812). German NT scholar. Griesbach was known for his significant contributions to the science of textual criticism, including his corrections to the *Textus Receptus, and for coining the label *Synoptic Gospels. *See also* Griesbach-Farmer Hypothesis.

Griesbach-Farmer Hypothesis. A theory on the composition of the Gospels that states that Matthew, rather than Mark, was the earliest Gospel to be written, and that Matthew was used by Mark and Luke to compose their Gospels. This theory was initially proposed by J. J. *Griesbach, fell into disfavor with scholars, but then was revived by William Farmer. *See also* Augustinian Hypothesis; Four-Source Hypothesis; Two-Source Hypothesis.

Gunkel, Hermann (1862-1932). German scholar of the *Religionsgeschichtliche Schule* and pioneer of *form criticism. Gunkel initially worked out his form-critical method in two influential commentaries on Genesis, then later on the Psalms. Gunkel sought to show that the OT stories and poems took shape originally in the *oral tradition of the people, before these works were written, expanded and edited in a later period. *See also* Mowinckel, Sigmund (1884-1965).

H

haggadah. A designation for the nonlegal content of the *Talmud and *midrashim (the Hebrew word means "narration" or "recital"). These comments, including moral teaching, theological speculation, stories, sayings, prayers, and the like, seek to explain a problem in the text or have the text speak to a new situation. In modern usage, haggadah (also spelled aggadah) comes to refer to the service for Passover. See also *halakah.

Hagiographa. *See* Ketubim.

halakah. The legal judgments of *rabbinic Judaism that function as definitive or binding rulings (the Hebrew term means "walk"), pointing the way for all aspects of Jewish practice (cf. Ex 18:20). The tradition of legal judgments begins in the Bible itself with Deuteronomy ("Second Law"), which functions as a "commentary" on the preceding laws in the *Pentateuch. It was carried forward with Ezra and the scribal traditions after the *Babylonian exile and codified by the rabbis in the *Talmud. The process of legal judgments on Jewish life and practices continues through commentaries and other writings. Thus, halakah is the ongoing application of *Torah.

Hammurabi, Code of. The most extensive of the law codes uncovered from the ancient Near East. Hammurabi was king of Babylon in the mid-eighteenth century B.C. The Code of Hammurabi appears to be an amalgamation and reform of existing laws. The laws cover civil and criminal issues, and the code contains a prologue and epilogue describing its provenance. The influence of the Code of Hammurabi in the ancient Near East is evident, since copies have been found throughout the region and from different periods. Its similarities in form and content with the biblical laws are noteworthy, but also noteworthy are the differences, especially the setting of the biblical laws as part of the exodus and *covenant at Sinai and the motive clauses for many of the laws. *See also* casuistic law; Torah.

hapax legomenon. A Greek expression (pl. *hapax legomena)* meaning something said only once. A certain word, for example, may occur only once in all of Paul's letters and be called a *hapax legomenon.* The concept has become important in considering the authorship of certain Pauline letters where a high number of *hapax legomena* in a document might suggest that Paul was not the actual author. Ephesians, for example, contains fifty-one *hapax legomena,* words not found in the undisputed letters of Paul.

haplography. A manuscript copyist's error of omitting a letter, word or phrase, often in instances when similar letters, words or phrases are adjacent to one another (contrast with *dittography). For example, in 1 Samuel 9:16, the *Masoretic Text reads, "I have seen my people," whereas the *Septuagint reads, "I have seen the affliction of my people." Since this is the third occurrence of "my people" in the verse, and since "affliction of" shares some similar letters with "my people," some scholars suggest that "affliction of" was inadvertently omitted in the transmission of the text (the phrase "affliction of my people" also occurs in Ex 3:7). A number of NT Greek manuscripts omit one of the two phrases, "has the Father," found in 1 John 2:23. Two long omissions in Matthew 5:19-20 may be due to the repetition of "the kingdom of heaven," which occurs three times in these verses. *See also* homoioteleuton; textual criticism.

harmony (of the Gospels). A work that seeks to harmonize the four Gospel accounts. Sometimes "harmony" is used synonymously with *synopsis of the Gospels or a Gospel parallel, but the function of a harmony is to interrelate the four Gospel accounts into a single continuous story of Jesus. A synopsis is a tool for the critical study of the Gospels that sets out the various *pericopes of Matthew, Mark and Luke (and sometimes John) in parallel columns for detailed comparison and analysis. As far as we know, Tatian's *Diatessaron* (c. 170) was the earliest attempt to provide a harmony of the Gospels.

Harnack, Adolf von (1851-1930). German church historian, theologian and biblical exegete. Harnack attempted to free *exegesis from the dogmatic and confessional affirmations of the church by stripping away the "husk" in order to uncover the "kernel" of the *gospel. He probably is best know for his popular book, *What Is Christianity* (1900), where he affirmed that the essence of Jesus' teaching can be reduced to the fatherhood of God, the kinship of humanity and the infinite value of the human soul. His scholarly work is illustrated by his three-volume *History of Dogma* (1880-1889; ET, 1896-1899).

Hasidim. In ancient Judaism, a group that opposed *Hellenism during the Hasmonean revolt (1 Macc 2:42-48). In more recent times the Hasidim was a Jewish renewal movement begun in the mid-eighteenth century in Eastern Europe (the Hebrew term means "pious ones"). It generally refers to anyone who faithfully follows *halakah, the legal judgments for Jews as a whole. Hasidic literature, especially the *homiletic stories, is very popular even beyond Jewish or religious readers.

Hasmoneans, Hasmonean dynasty. The family name of the *Maccabean priestly and kingly family who ruled over Israel from the 160s B.C. until the Romans captured Jerusalem in 63 B.C. The story of the Hasmoneans is told in 1 and 2 Maccabees. The name "Hasmonean" is not used in those texts, but it is used by *Josephus, our other important historical source for the events that led to the Hasmonean rule. The name seems to come from an older ancestral name, *Hašmônay* (Gk *Asmōnaios* in Josephus). Under the Hasmonean dynasty the kingdom of Judah extended its borders to an extent equal to the borders that King David established during his reign. In the end the Hasmonean dynasty fell prey to the competing factions that had emerged in the region under its rule, and, of course, the power of the new Roman Empire that brought "peace" to a region that the *Hellenistic rulers had been unable to maintain. *See also pax Romana*.

Hauptbriefe. A German term (literally "head" or "primary" letters) commonly referring to four letters of Paul: Romans, 1 and 2 Corinthians and Galatians. This term should not be confused with the list of seven letters widely regarded today as "authentic" Pauline letters, which would include Philippians, 1 Thessalonians and Philemon with the four *Hauptbriefe* (although in the more radical perspective of F. C. *Baur, the four *Hauptbriefe* were indeed the only authentic letters of Paul). *See also* deutero-Pauline; Pauline homologoumena.

Haustafeln. See household code.

Hebrew Bible. The OT. The term *Hebrew Bible* has been employed in recent years as an attempt both to be descriptive and to display greater respect for Judaism, since "Old Testament" carries connotations of being superseded by the NT. Some scholars, however, argue that the terms OT and NT show the importance of the death and resurrection of Jesus Christ, and therefore the distinction between old and new still has a place in Christian theology. *See also* Tanak.

Heilsgeschichte. German term usually translated as "salvation history" or "redemptive history." See also Cullmann, Oscar; salvation history.

Hellenism, hellenization. The cultural influences beginning with Alexander the Great (334 B.C.), in which Greek culture (ideas, customs, government, architecture, language, religion, etc.) spread throughout the Mediterranean world and was embraced by many non-Greek cultures and societies. Palestine, for example, was "hellenized" to a large extent during this time. Most Jews living in the *Diaspora were identified as "Hellenistic Jews" because they spoke Greek, adopted many Greek customs and used the *Septuagint as their Scriptures (see "Hellenists" in Acts 6:1). *See also* *Hellenistic Judaism.

Hellenistic Judaism. A designation for a type of Judaism (or Judaisms) that embraced many values of Greek culture and language. *Philo of Alexandria (c. 20 B.C.-c. A.D. 50), for example, was a Hellenistic Jewish scholar who sought to interpret the OT by utilizing Greek philosophy and *allegorical exegesis. The apostle Paul was a Hellenistic Jew because he was born and raised in the Jewish-Hellenistic city of Tarsus (*see* Hellenism). It is important to recognize that all Jews during the intertestamental period were influenced by Greek culture in some way, so that Hellenistic Judaism designates various degrees of acceptance.

henotheism. Commitment to one god without denying the existence of other gods. This belief seems to be evidenced at times in the religion of the *patriarchs and their families and probably existed into the later history of Israel in popular culture. For example, Micah 4:5 reads, "For all the peoples walk, each in the name of its god, but we will walk in the name of the LORD our God forever and ever."

hermeneutics. The discipline that studies theories of interpretation. The term *hermeneutics* was first used with respect to interpretive methods and discussions of biblical interpretation; now the term has a broader use as the theory and art of interpreting any text. This broader philosophical consideration of hermeneutics has introduced some tensions into more traditional modes of interpreting biblical texts, but it also has produced fruitful discussions on the act of reading generally, the nature and authority of texts, and the relationship between theory and practice. *See also* exegesis.

Hexapla. *Origen's six-column arrangement (in the third century A.D.) of the various Greek translations of the Old Testament alongside the Hebrew text and Origen's own transliteration of the Hebrew into Greek letters. Except for fragments, this text has been lost, though greater portions of it survive in the Syro-Hexapla, a Syriac translation of Origen's work dating to the seventh century

A.D. The Hexapla gives important evidence for the state of the Hebrew text during the *patristic era. *See also* Septuagint; textual criticism.

Hexateuch. The first six books of the Old Testament, viewed as an integrated literary entity. Some scholars argue that the book of Joshua belongs with the *Pentateuch, thus making six *(hex)* books rather than the five of the traditional division. These six books have a unity based on *form-critical considerations (e.g., the repetition of brief *creeds; cf. Deut 26:5-11 with Josh 24:1-28) and the inclusion of the conquest traditions that complete the promise of land to Abraham. However, the canonical role of the *Pentateuch testifies to another unity that should not be overlooked, one where the fundamentals of biblical faith are set forth in election, *covenant, law and deliverance. *See also* Pentateuch; Torah.

hieroglyph. A pictorial script. Derived from the Greek term meaning "priestly sign," hieroglyphs originally referred to Egyptian religious writings. But it also came to be used for any pictorial script. Using pictures to represent objects can easily become cumbersome due to the sheer volume of signs necessary. The "rebus principle," where a sign is read for a sound rather than a meaning, eventually expanded the range of writing and led to the alphabetic system of writing that most cultures use today.

higher criticism. A term that refers to the critical study of biblical texts, especially the evaluation of questions such as authorship, date, sources and composition. The term originated with J. G. *Eichhorn and was contrasted with *textual, or *lower, criticism. Among conservative interpreters, the term *higher criticism* frequently implied the imposition of modern, "scientific" presuppositions upon the study of Scripture. These terms are no longer widely used by scholars. See historical criticism.

Hillel. A prominent rabbi of the late first century B.C. and early first century A.D. Hillel the Elder was roughly contemporary with Jesus and Paul, and in rabbinic tradition he was regarded as the most influential person in postbiblical Jewish history, often being compared to Moses and Ezra. Tradition claims that he was a leader of the Pharisees (30 B.C.—10 A.D.) as well as president of the Sanhedrin. His views of the law were carried on by his followers (the house or school of Hillel) and prevailed after the destruction of

Jerusalem in A.D. 70. *See also* Shammai.

historical criticism. An approach to the text that seeks to determine "what really happened." The *historical-critical method* refers to the effort to reconstruct the historical context and meaning of a text. Typically this approach answers questions about the *origin* of texts (*see* source criticism) rather than the final form (*see* canonical criticism). It also seeks to find the *original meaning* of a text, what a text meant to the first readers rather than subsequent or modern readers. The "true" meaning of a passage is the meaning of the words in their historical context, not what the church or some other authority might say regarding a text. This final point about authority is the driving force behind historical criticism: historical critics sought a scholarship without prejudice, beliefs or creeds; they sought to be *neutral observers* regarding the meaning of a text. Historical criticism has come under criticism itself in recent years for a variety of reasons, not the least of which is that its adherents have not been historical or critical enough. Also, the whole issue of "neutrality" in interpretation is severely criticized in the light of postmodern concerns about how we read texts (*see* deconstruction; reader-response criticism). Nevertheless, historical criticism is invaluable in saying what a text *can* or *cannot* mean, rather than what it *did* mean. It can be a corrective to abuses of interpretation, or it can limit the range of interpretations. However, to say that a text *means* one thing only begs a question of what purposes one has in reading a text, and a "historical" purpose is not the only purpose one might have in reading a text. *See also* typology.

historical Jesus. *See* Quest of the Historical Jesus.

Historie, historisch. In German theology, particularly in the writings of Rudolf *Bultmann on Jesus and the Gospels, important distinctions were made between several concepts in German that are very difficult to distinguish in English. "History" (German *Historie*; adj. *historisch)* is used to describe historically objective facts (dates, places, etc.) that can be verified through study and research, such as, "Jesus was a Jew who lived in the first century." *Geschichte*, on the other hand, is used to indicate events of historic significance, claims that are historically (in the *historisch* sense) nonverifiable, such as "Jesus is the Son of God." Martin Kahler's famous book title, *The So-Called Historical [historische] Jesus and the Historic [geschichtliche] Bib-*

lical Christ played the two terms off one another.

history of religions school. A late nineteenth and early twentieth century "school" (German *Schule)* or scholarly movement that sought to interpret Judaism and Christianity in terms of their broader religious environment and historical legacy. These scholars, who were mostly German (such as H. *Gunkel, W. Bousset, R. Reitzenstein, W. *Wrede, R. *Bultmann, W. Heitmüller), argued that Judaism and Christianity borrowed concepts, language and practices from other religious movements. So, for example, early Christian christology was indebted to a pre-Christian *gnostic "primal man" myth, and there were antecedents for Christian baptism in the *mystery religions. This movement is also known as the *Religionsgeschichtliche Schule.*

Hittite. People of Indo-European origin whose influence spread from Asia Minor throughout the *Levant during the second millennium B.C. The Hittites appear in the stories of the *Patriarchs (Gen 23), the conquest of Canaan (Judg 3:5-6) and even during the monarchy (2 Sam 11—12). Hittite treaties are considered by some scholars to be the model for the OT *covenant.

Holiness Code. A designation given by scholars to the laws found in Leviticus 17—26. Some scholars posit that these laws circulated independently of the Pentateuch and were written perhaps in the late monarchical period. The label Holiness Code derives from the refrain, "You shall be holy, for I the LORD your God am holy" (Lev 19:2, etc.). According to the *Documentary Hypothesis, the Holiness Code comes from the *Priestly source.

holy war. The total devotion to *Yahweh for holocaust or sacrifice (Heb *ḥērem)* of every person, all livestock and goods taken in battle, especially during the conquest of Canaan after the exodus from Egypt (cf. Deut 7:1-2). Joshua 6 is the prime example of holy war carried out by the Israelites. Since war was an ever-present threat and reality in the ancient world, the term *holy war* is also used by scholars to underscore the fact that warfare was not exclusively political but entailed the religious life and practices of the Israelites and other peoples. In Israel, holy war was tied to the *covenant relationship, which is political and *cultic; religious rituals were enacted in preparation and conduct of war (Deut 20). The notion of holy war, however, should not be taken to mean that the ancient

Israelites thought that Yahweh always fought on their behalf since, if they did not live according to the covenant, the Israelites could experience Yahweh's judgment by means of wars from foreign invaders.

homiletics. The discipline that deals with the preparation, structure and delivery of sermons (*homilies).

homily. Another term for a sermon or a discourse given within the context of worship in the Jewish *synagogue (Acts 13:13-41) or early church. Its focus is upon exhortation and the interpretation of Scripture for believers rather than the proclamation (*kerygma) of the *gospel to unbelievers. Some scholars suggest that early Christian homilies may be embedded in certain books of the NT, such as Ephesians, Hebrews and James.

homoioteleuton. Literally, "similar ending." In copying manuscripts, similar endings were often the occasion for errors of eyesight, in which words or even entire lines were omitted. An example is John 17:15 in the manuscript Codex Vaticanus, where a scribe omits an entire line of the text. *See also* dittography; haplography; textual criticism.

homologoumena. In *Eusebius's categories of the NT canon, those NT books confessed by the church as Scripture. For Eusebius, the homologoumena (Gk *homologeō*, "to confess, acknowledge publicly"), the writings acknowledged as Scripture by the church of his day, included the four Gospels, Acts, fourteen letters of Paul (including Hebrews), 1 Peter, 1 John and perhaps Revelation. *See also* antilegomena; Pauline homologoumena.

Hort, F. J. A. (1828-1892). Notable British textual critic. Much of Hort's work is associated with his colleague, B. F. *Westcott, with whom he collaborated on an important critical text of the Greek NT, *The New Testament in the Original Greek, with Introduction and Appendix* (1881). He was a major contributor to the English Revised Version of 1881.

hortatory. Teaching characterized by the giving of advice or exhortation. *See also* paraenesis.

household code. "Rules" or "tables" found in the NT and Greek literature that deal with domestic relationships between husband and wife, children and parents, slaves and masters, in the home or church (Eph 5:21—6:9; Col 3:18—4:1; 1 Pet 2:18—3:7). In many respects, the NT rules conform to the social structures of the first century, but because they are Christian, they incorporate principles of mutual responsibility, respect, love and sincerity. The German term, *Haustafeln,* is often used in NT studies and commentaries.

hymn. Praise to God either describing a turn of fortune from sickness or danger to deliverance or victory, or simply recounting God's majesty and goodness. Of the two most common forms of OT psalms (hymns and *laments), hymns have the less complicated form. Based upon style, structure, content and mood, hymns have a threefold form, while laments have a sixfold form. Hymns begin with a call to praise, followed by the reason(s) for the praise, and concluding with a return to the initial call to praise. Psalm 117, the briefest psalm, is a good example of a hymn. Each of the five books of the *Psalter ends with a hymn, and the Psalter as a whole ends with five hymns. The Hebrew designation of the Psalter is *sēpher tᵉhillîm,* which means "book of praises," an appropriate name for hymnic material. Hymns can include *thanksgivings, royal psalms, *enthronement psalms, and any psalm that shares forms similar to the basic pattern of the hymn. Hymns are found outside the Psalter, as, for example, in the Song of Moses (Ex 15). Hymns are also found in the NT, where the most significant ones are found in Luke's Gospel (*Magnificat, 1:46-55; *Benedictus, 1:68-79; Gloria, 2:14; *Nunc Dimittis, 2:29-32). Other passages in the NT indicate that singing, in the form of psalms, hymns and spiritual songs (1 Cor 14:26; Eph 5:19; Col 3:16), was a significant part of early Christian worship. Scholars have identified certain passages in the NT (Eph 1:3-14; Phil 2:6-11; Col 1:15-20; 1 Tim 3:16) as hymnic material.

I

Ibn Ezra (1092/1093-1167). Jewish interpreter known for his erudition and attention to the "plain meaning" (*peshat) of the text. His comments, especially on Isaiah and *Torah, anticipated many of the modern concerns of commentators. *See also* Isaiah, multiple authorship of; Documentary Hypothesis.

Ignatius, St. (c. A.D. 35-107). An early church father, bishop of Antioch. He wrote a number of letters to churches in Asia Minor as well as one to Rome, where he was martyred by Emperor Trajan. His letters reveal several developments in Christian theology from the apostolic period to the second century A.D.

implied author. A term in narrative criticism that distinguishes the persona that is presented in the text from the real author. The implied author is a creation of the real author, and the character of the implied author is implied and embedded in the text. The implied author writes to an *implied reader. In some cases the term *implied author* is used when the authorship of a certain document is questioned. Scholars who doubt the Pauline authorship of Ephesians, for example, might choose to speak of the implied author rather than Paul.

implied reader. A term in narrative criticism that distinguishes the reader implied in a text from the real reader. The implied reader is the profile of the reader who would best understand and respond to the text, sometimes called the ideal reader. Even where the readers are identified as "all the saints in Christ Jesus . . . in Philippi" (Phil 1:1), narrative criticism will carefully read the text for indications of the implied reader of the text. This is more profitable in reading Ephesians, where we cannot be sure whether the real readers are actually linked with a particular church in Ephesus or with the surrounding regions. More commonly, narrative texts, such as the Fourth Gospel, invite readers to detect the implied reader.

imprecatory psalms. Psalms that call upon God to destroy the enemies of God's people, also referred to as psalms of cursing or vengeance. Imprecatory psalms are disturbing or even repulsive to some modern readers (e.g., Ps 137:9: "Happy shall they be who take your [Babylonian] little ones and dash them against the rock"). Some people excise these verses by omitting them in their reading or use of the Psalms, especially in worship, or argue that they have been superseded by the NT's call to love one's enemies. Others see these psalms as honest expressions of deep emotions and argue that as *prayers to God,* they allow the psalmist to give over his or her anger to God. In this latter view, God will deal with the enemies in his justice and mercy, so the possibility exists for reconciliation and restoration.

inclusio. A technical literary term referring to a framing or bracketing (Latin "confinement"), where the opening phrase or idea in a passage is repeated at the end. For example, Psalm 8 begins (v. 1) and ends (v. 9) with "O LORD, our Sovereign, how majestic is your name in all the earth" (cf. Ps 1; Ezek 25:3-7; Amos 1:3-5), thus reinforcing the importance of the words.

inner-biblical exegesis. An approach to the text that seeks to address the re-interpretation and reapplication of earlier biblical texts by later texts. The detection of inner-biblical exegesis is more developed in OT studies, largely due to the monumental study by M. Fishbane, *Biblical Interpretation in Ancient Israel* (1985). Direct quotations are the most obvious application of this method, but inner-biblical exegesis also looks at *glosses in a text, the arrangement of material in its present form, and the use of words, themes and traditions in other texts. For example, a scholar studying inner-biblical exegesis might examine the relationship of Isaiah 2:2-4 to Joel 3:10 and Micah 4:1-3, or the use that Hosea puts to the traditions of Genesis 32 regarding Isaac and Esau. This approach to texts shares features with interpreting "Scripture in the light of Scripture" but focuses more on the literary and historical relationships rather than the theological or spiritual ones. Some scholars use the term "comparative midrash" as roughly equivalent to inner-biblical exegesis. *See also* intertextuality.

intertextuality. The phenomenon that all texts are involved in an interplay with other texts, which results in the interpretive principle that no text can be viewed as isolated and independent. This interplay is particularly true of biblical literature, since each document, or text, is self-consciously part of a stream of tradition. The study of intertextuality pays attention to the fragments, or "echoes," of earlier texts that appear in later texts, examining texts that share words and themes. Generally the study of biblical intertextuality focuses more on the *processes* by which biblical texts were reworked and the *differences* between the texts: texts were extended in meaning but also transposed or even refuted. The emphasis tends toward exploring the *plurality* of possible readings rather than the *conformity* of readings. *See also* inner-biblical exegesis.

ipsissima verba Jesu. Latin for "the very words of Jesus." Scholars have attempted to uncover within the Gospels the authentic sayings of Jesus. *Ipsissima verba Jesu* designates those words that are most certain to have been spoken by Jesus. *See also* criteria of authenticity; *ipsissima vox Jesu.*

ipsissima vox Jesu. Latin for "the very voice of Jesus." A scholar may conclude that although the words of Jesus in question may not be his very words (******ipsissima verba*), they accurately express his mind, intentions and meaning; that is, one hears in them the very "voice" of Jesus. *See also* criteria of authenticity; *ipsissima verba Jesu.*

Irenaeus (c. 135-c. 202). Early Christian father. Born in Smyrna in Asia Minor, Irenaeus was later made bishop of Lyons and traveled throughout the Roman Empire. During the last quarter of the second century, orthodox Christianity was contending with *Gnosticism for the hearts and minds of the people. Irenaeus's major work was *Adversus haereses (Against Heresies)*, in which he challenged the *gnostics for their false interpretation of Scripture. For Irenaeus, true interpretation conforms to the "church's rule of faith," its witness to Christ and its conformity to the apostolic preaching.

irony. A statement in which the implicit meaning of the words differs from the explicit use of those words. When Elijah says to the prophets of Baal on Mt. Carmel, "Cry aloud! Surely he is a god; either he is meditating, or he has wandered away, or he is on a journey, or perhaps he is asleep and must be awakened" (1 Kings 18:27), he is being ironic—he does not believe that their gods are gods at all, and they will not pass the test. The danger of irony is that it will be missed. The book of Jonah, by most accounts, is an ironical treatment of justice (and grace); it is a story of Jonah, not the oracles of Jonah such as we find in the other prophetic books. The problem of many contemporary treatments of irony in the Bible is that irony, that "catless grin" (H. Davenport), is discerned everywhere and can mean merely something unintended or simply odd. This problem is especially acute in our current crisis, where authorial intent is disparaged. To be able to find irony in a text, the reader must be able to trust what is said and to discern a reason why what is said is not what is intended. In the NT Jesus uses irony when dealing with the scribes and Pharisees in Matthew 23 (especially v. 32), and Paul resorts to irony in his discussions with the Corinthians (cf. 1 Cor 3—4).

Isaiah, multiple authorship of. The problem of multiple authorship and the composition of the book of Isaiah. Critical scholarship of the late eighteenth century posited three Isaiahs based upon differing styles, themes and settings (though as early as medieval times, commentators such as in *Ibn Ezra noted the differences in style). First Isaiah was the Isaiah of Jerusalem, writing in the eighth century B.C.; Second Isaiah (Deutero-Isaiah) was identified with chapters 40—55, where an *exilic setting was envisioned; Third Isaiah (Trito-Isaiah), identified with chapters 56—66, reflected themes of a postexilic setting in the land of Israel. Many scholars who hold to multiple authorship no longer emphasize the differences and individuality of the three "Isaiahs"; rather, they argue how the parts contribute to a literary whole, especially how themes are picked up and used in later contexts.

J

Jamnia, Council of. *Rabbinic council held at Jamnia (also spelled Yavneh), in Palestine. When the Jews fled from Jerusalem during the First Jewish Revolt (A.D. 66—70), many went to Jamnia, a town on the coastal plain of ancient Palestine, south of Joppa, under the leadership of Rabbi Yohanan ben Zakkai. An academy was established there, and through meetings over several years many issues concerning the reconstruction of Judaism were discussed. (Many scholars now doubt that a "council" was held, but certainly discussions took place.) For Christians, the discussions regarding the books of the *Hebrew Bible were the most important, since these discussions led to the eventual "canonization" of the third section, the *Writings, of the Hebrew Scriptures. *See also* canon.

Jahwist. According to the *Documentary Hypothesis, the author of the J source in the Pentateuch who prefers the name *Yahweh* when referring to God. The letter J comes from the German spelling of Yahweh, *Jahve*. *See also* Documentary Hypothesis; Yahwist.

JEDP. *See* Documentary Hypothesis.

Jeremias, Joachim (1900-1979). German NT scholar. Jeremias spent most of his academic career at the University of Göttingen (1935-1968). He strongly believed that the NT must be interpreted within the linguistic and historical setting of the first century and that the historical Jesus, as discovered in the Gospels, is important to Christian faith. Both of these convictions are adequately demonstrated in his *Eucharistic Words of Jesus* (ET, 1955), *New Testament Theology: The Proclamation of Jesus* (ET, 1971) and *Parables of Jesus* (ET, 1954).

Jerome (c. 347-420). Early church father and biblical scholar. Jerome was one of the most interesting and complex of the early church fathers, being without equal in breadth, depth and versatility of learning. Born to Christian parents in Italy, he went to Rome at the age of twelve to study Greek, Latin, rhetoric and philosophy. He later traveled east and studied Hebrew, eventually coming to Bethlehem, where he lived the remainder of his life. His method of interpretation was to set down his new translation of the Hebrew side by side with the *Septuagint and comment on each. He interpreted each verse literally by drawing upon his *rabbinic sources, then he interpreted each verse spiritually by utilizing the Septuagint and *Origen. Jerome's translation of the Hebrew and Greek Bible has come down to us as the *Vulgate.

Jerusalem Council. *See* Council of Jerusalem.

Jesus Seminar, the. A group of scholars (approximately fifty to seventy-five in number) who usually meet twice a year to debate questions about the historical Jesus. They are popularly known for their voting on the authenticity of Jesus' sayings according to a scale of probability. Different color codes correspond to each level: red to indicate that Jesus uttered a particular saying; pink for the possibility that Jesus said something like that; gray to signify that a saying is perhaps Jesus' idea but not his words; and black to indicate that Jesus did not say this. The group has also included the apocryphal *Gospel of Thomas* in their study. The result of their work has been published in *The Five Gospels: The Search for the Authentic Words of Jesus* (New York: Macmillan,1993).

Jesus tradition. The sayings and stories of Jesus as they were disseminated and passed down in *oral and written form. The term is used quite frequently in contemporary studies of Jesus in which scholars attempt to trace the development and identify the transformations of sayings or stories of Jesus as they were transmitted. This investigation includes questions such as whether and to what extent the writings of a Paul or James reveal access to the Jesus tradition. For some scholars, such as those of the *Jesus Seminar, the investigation moves beyond the canonical literature to include works such as the *Gospel of Thomas*. *See also* tradition criticism.

Jewish Christians. Jews who were disciples of Jesus or converted to Christianity by confessing Jesus as the Messiah and were baptized "into the name of Jesus" (Acts 2:38). Sometimes this group of early Jewish Christians is described as Palestinian Christians because the movement was largely confined to Palestine. It appears that Jewish Christians, under the leadership of James (Acts 15:1-35; 21:17-26), particularly those in and around Jerusalem, retained many of their Jewish traditions and beliefs—in other words, they continued to "live Jewishly" and saw no need to cease being Jews because they converted to Christianity. It is likely that some of these Jewish/Palestinian Christians, those called *Judaizers by modern authors, insisted that Paul require Gentile converts to obey Jewish laws in addition to putting their faith in Jesus Christ (Gal 2—3). *See also* Ebionites.

Jewish Revolt. The Jewish war against Rome in A.D. 66-70. Although there were a number of Jewish revolts against foreign powers throughout history (Assyrians, Babylonians, Greeks), the one most often referred to in biblical history is the one against Rome beginning in A.D. 66, which led to the destruction of Jerusalem and the temple in A.D. 70 under the Roman general Titus. A second revolt against Rome, known as the *Bar Kokhba Revolt, took place in A.D. 132-135. *See also* Zealots.

Johannine Comma. See Comma Johanneum.

Josephus. Jewish historian. Josephus lived in the first century (c. A.D. 37/38-110), and his works are an important source for understanding the historical and religious world of Palestine during the Roman rule. Josephus was pressed into service against the Romans by the Jewish forces in the Galilee, was taken prisoner, and later become a Roman citizen. His writings include an autobiography *(Life)*, an apologetic for Judaism *(Against Apion)*, a history of the Jews from the creation of the world until the Jewish war against Rome *(Antiquities of the Jews)* and an account of the war against Rome *(Jewish War)*. Some scholars doubt the reliability of his work, since he appears uncritical of his earlier sources, upon which he relies heavily; nevertheless, he remains an invaluable source of information about the community in Palestine during the *Hellenistic period. His writings were more prized by Christians than by Jews because he names John the Baptist and Jesus. We also learn much of what happened at Masada during the first *Jewish Revolt through his writings.

Jubilee, Year of. The year that concludes the cycle of seven sabbatical years in which "liberty" was proclaimed for all (people, chattel and land) and restoration to former positions was granted. Leviticus 25 sets forth regulations regarding ownership of land and slaves. Land and humans were not to be owned by other humans, for both belong to the Lord (24:23, 42). The soil was to have a "sabbath" every seven years, but in the fiftieth year (7x7+1), the land itself would be "released" back to its original owner. Similarly, a slave, someone indentured because of debt, could be released by a kinsman or by the occurrence of the Jubilee Year. The prophet Ezekiel also speaks about a year of "release" when property reverted back to its owner (Ezek 46:16-18), and the image is taken up in the NT as well when Jesus uses the words of Is 61:1-2 ("The spirit of the Lord GOD is upon me . . . to bring good news to the oppressed, to bind up the brokenhearted, . . . to proclaim the year of the LORD's favor") in the synagogue in Nazareth (cf. Lk 4:18-19).

Judaizers. A group of Jewish Christians who believed that all Gentile Christians should "live like Jews" (Gal 2:14) by embracing Jewish customs. Although the word *Judaizer* does not appear in the NT, such attempts at "judaizing" conflicted with Paul's insistence that salvation is "not by the works of the law but through faith in Jesus Christ" (Gal 2:16). It is important to understand that Paul never encouraged *Jewish Christians to abandon their Jewish way of life and national identity, though he was falsely accused of doing so (Acts 21:21).

Justin Martyr (c. 100-165). The first great apologist of the church. Justin's *First Apology*, written from Rome about A.D. 155 to the emperor Antonius Pius (138-161), presented and interpreted the Christian faith by addressing the false charges of immorality leveled against the church. In his other works, Justin sought to reconcile the claims of faith and reason. He, along with some of his disciples, were denounced as Christians and were executed because they refused to sacrifice to Rome.

K

Käsemann, Ernst (1906-1998). German NT scholar. Käsemann had a long teaching tenure at the University of Tübingen. Although he was a pupil of *Bultmann, he differed with his mentor on a number of issues, including the *quest for the historical Jesus. Käsemann, along with other post-Bultmannians (*Bornkamm, *Conzelmann, Ebeling, Fuchs), sought to form a bridge between the earthly Jesus and the Jesus proclaimed by the church. The theology of Paul, especially the doctrines of justification and righteousness, and the centrality of the cross (*theologia crucis) are central features of Käsemann's work.

kenosis. The "emptying" of Christ in his incarnation. The Greek verb *kenoō* ("to empty") occurs in the Christ-hymn in Philippians 2:6-11, which states that Christ "emptied *(ekenōsen)* himself, taking the form of a slave" (Phil 2:7). The christological problem that emerged over the interpretation of this verse centers on the question of whether "emptied" means that Jesus temporarily "gave up" the exercise of certain divine *prerogatives* or whether he gave up certain divine *attributes*.

kerygma. From the Greek noun *kērygma*, signifying what is preached (verb, *kēryssō*) as the *gospel. Kerygma thus stands for the content as well as the act of preaching (1 Cor 1:21). Some contemporary NT scholars continue to follow or modify C. H. *Dodd's proposal that the basic content of the kerygma declared that: (1) the messianic age foretold by the prophets has arrived; (2) the fulfillment of the messianic age is demonstrated by the life, death and resurrection of Jesus; (3) by virtue of his resurrection, Jesus is the exalted Lord; (4) the presence of the Holy Spirit in the church is a sign of God's presence with his people; (5) Christ will return as Judge and Savior of the world; and (6) the call to repentance includes an offer of forgiveness from sins and the reception of the Holy Spirit as a guarantee of salvation.

Ketubim. The third section of the Hebrew *canon (also spelled Ketuvim), the *Writings (also referred to by its Latin name, *hagiographa*). This section comprises Psalms, Job, Proverbs, the "Festival Books" (Hebrew *Megilloth: Ruth, Song of Solomon, Ecclesiastes, Lamentations and Esther), Daniel, Ezra, Nehemiah and 1 and 2 Chronicles. *See also* Tanak.

kingdom of God. God's rule over the people of God and the entire created order. During the *second temple period, Jewish thought regarding the kingdom focused on God becoming King and vindicating the Jewish nation by vanquishing their enemies and ushering in a period of peace. The kingdom (reign) of God was a major focus in Jesus' teaching (Mt 6:33; Mk 1:5; Lk 6:20) where the kingdom is present in the person and teaching of Jesus (Lk 10:9; 17:21) even though it awaits a future consummation (Lk 13:29; 22:18).

kinsman redeemer. *See* levirate marriage.

Kittel, Gerhard (1888-1948). German scholar known primarily for editing the nine-volume *Theologisches Wörterbuch zum Neuen Testament* (1933-73), translated into English by Geoffrey W. Bromiley as *Theological Dictionary of the New Testament* (1964-74).

Koheleth. Hebrew name for Ecclesiastes. *See also* Qoheleth.

Koine. The common Greek language of the NT era (as opposed, e.g., to the Attic Greek of the classical era) and the type of Greek used by the NT writers.

koinōnia. A Greek word meaning "fellowship, partnership, a sharing in." Luke indicates that *koinōnia* was one of the distinguishing marks of the early church, where it was experienced in worship, particularly by sharing in "the breaking of bread" (Acts 2:42).

Kultgeschichtliche Schule. *See* Myth and Ritual School.

kyrios. A Greek term translated as "Lord, master, owner, sir," when used as a form of address. In NT theology, it is a title given to Jesus as a consequence of his resurrection and exaltation: "God has made him [Jesus] both Lord *[kyrios]* and Messiah *[christos]*" (Acts 2:36). It became the common term to express Christ's lordship in the Greco-Roman world (Rom 10:9; Phil 2:11). *See also* christological titles.

L

L tradition. Gospel material that is uniquely found in Luke's Gospel. In B. H. Streeter's proposal of the *Four-Source Hypothesis, L signifies material that is unique to Luke's Gospel, such as the parables of the Good Samaritan (Lk 10:29-37) and the Prodigal Son (15:11-32).

lament psalms. A complaint or request to God by an individual or the community because of suffering, oppression or perhaps even negligence from God. Laments, perhaps better rendered as "complaint" (German, *klage*), are one of two basic forms of psalms (*hymns and laments) that are distinguished on the basis of style, structure, content and mood. Laments have a more complicated structure than hymns. Laments begin with a call to God, then follow with a description of the need or complaint, a request for help, the reasons God should intervene, a statement of trust, and a concluding praise. Laments encompass dirges and complaints, among other *genres. Psalm 13 is a beautiful and brief example of a lament.

Lasterkatalog. *See* catalogue of vices and virtues.

Latinism. A word or grammatical construction derived from Latin. Latinisms are found in the NT, particularly in the Gospels and Acts (Gk, *kenturiōn* / Lat, *centurion*; Gk, *praitōrion* / Lat *praetorium*). Biblical interpretation is suffused with Latinisms. For example, the word **lexicon* (dictionary) is derived from the Latin *lexis*, "word."

Latter Prophets. *See* Nebiim.

lectionary. From the Latin word for "a reader," a collection of readings ("lections") of Scripture and other liturgical materials used in public worship and private devotion. Lectionaries, often arranged and used according to ecclesiastical and secular calendars, originated in the early church. Among other things, the early Christian lectionaries provide useful evidence for scholars seeking to reconstruct the early Greek text of the Bible.

legend. A literary *genre similar to *saga but focusing more on the *character* and *gifts* of the central person in the story. Legends tend toward exhortation, calling readers to a course of action. For example, the stories of Joseph or Daniel in foreign courts focus on the character of these individuals and call for faithfulness and wisdom in dire situations. When scholars speak of a story as a legend, they are not necessarily judging its historicity; they are primarily speaking of its genre. *See* etiology.

Leitmotiv. A German word that refers to an image, quality, action or object that recurs through a narrative, poem or oracle (literally, "leading motif/theme"). The *Leitmotiv* may be symbolic, but it may also give coherence to a narrative and sustain a basic theme of the story. For example, in the stories of the *patriarchs the motifs of the younger supplanting the elder or the wife being passed off as a sister are incorporated into the narrative art and contribute to the meaning of the story. In the case of the younger supplanting the elder, it is not primacy of birth but the promise and purpose of God that determines through whom the blessings of God will come. *See also* literary criticism; *Leitwort.*

Leitwort. A word that recurs significantly in a *pericope or an extended story, poem or oracle (literally, from the German, "leading word"). By following the repetition of the word and the different uses that occur, an interpreter can grasp a text's meaning, sometimes with striking results. In the OT, it is not simply a word, but the root form and variations on that root that can be exploited to express shades of meaning. For example, in the aftermath of the flood, the word-stem "live" is repeated in various forms, highlighting both the destruction and the rescue or renewal of life (Gen 6:9—8:19). *See also* literary criticism; *Leitmotiv.*

Levant. The coastal lands of the Eastern Mediterranean Sea (which include Palestine/Israel, Syria and Lebanon). Situated around the Syrian Desert, the Levant was important for both Egypt and Mesopotamia to control, since it was the only land mass through which trade could reasonably be conducted. *See also* Fertile Crescent.

levirate marriage. An institution in ancient Israel that preserved the inheritance rights of a man who had died childless. In the event of a man's death, the eldest brother's obligation was to marry the widow and have a child who would carry on the "name" and become the heir of the deceased husband (Deut 25:5-10). The institution also provided status for the widow. The book of Ruth presupposes the institution (Ruth 3:13); Boaz "redeemed" both the field and Ruth, so "kinsman redeemer" was sometimes used of the person. The story also suggests that simple inheritance was not the sole issue, since both Naomi and Ruth were more concerned with life within the community than with the rights established by the social structures, although rights would be a natural outgrowth of the "new" social status (Ruth 4:1-10).

lexicon. In biblical studies, the common designation for a dictionary of Hebrew, Greek or Latin words.

lex talionis. A Latin term meaning "law of retribution." The term is typically applied to OT laws that embody a "fixed ratio" principle of justice not based on status or money but on *kind:* "an eye for an eye, a tooth for a tooth." Although this seems a harsh form of punishment, one should keep in mind that the penalty was not specified on the basis of status, but applied equally to all (in contrast to, e.g., the *Hammurabi Code). It limited the punishment by not exacting a greater amount in retribution. It was a *legal principle,* not a principle for interpersonal relationships.

libertinism. *See* antinomian.

Lightfoot, J. B. (1828-1889). British NT scholar. Lightfoot was bishop of Durham and was known for his hermeneutical passion to interpret the text of the Bible within the context of the languages and cultures of the time in which they were written. In addition to being a brilliant scholar, he championed many causes for the church, such as lay ministries and female participation in church leadership. His essay "The Christian Ministry" in his commentary on *St. Paul's Epistle to the Philippians* (1897) remains a timeless statement on this topic.

literary criticism. An approach to the biblical text that recognizes its literary nature and seeks to interpret it as such. The literary critic seeks to interpret the *whole* of the literary work, whether a psalm, a story that goes on for several chapters (e.g., the story of Jacob or Joseph) or a book (Job). Its aim is to see the parts in terms of the whole, not just as individual parts. Many literary critics go so far as to say that the literary work should be interpreted in and of itself without reference to any historical reconstruction. The work itself contains most, if not all, of the necessary information for interpreting it. For example, the story of Hosea's marriage to Gomer can be seen as a *parable for the relationship between God and his people and need not be taken as a "historical" marriage, with its implicit problem of explaining the "uncomfortable" situation of God asking Hosea to marry a prostitute. Discussions of plot, characterization and themes hold interest for the literary critic, not questions of authorship and date of composition. The danger of some forms of literary criticism is in losing sight of the historical grounding of these stories. The testimony of these stories is that God is acting in these events and lives; they are not simply plots and characters acting out their destiny. Older literary approaches, still widely employed, seek to show how a literary composition came to be and what sources underlie the present work. *See also* historical criticism; source criticism.

locus classicus. A Latin term meaning "classical place." In biblical studies, *locus classicus* refers to a passage of Scripture that best illustrates a principle, doctrine or understanding of a biblical idea. For example, Micah 6:8—"What does the LORD require of you but to do justice, and to love kindness, and to walk humbly with your God?"—is a crucial passage for understanding what God requires in the *covenant relationship under *Torah. Similarly, Deuteronomy 18:15-22 is a passage that best states what a true prophet was to be. In the NT, Jesus' quotation of the OT in Luke 10:27 is a *locus classicus* for Christian discipleship: "You shall love the Lord your God with all your heart, and with all your soul, and with all your strength, and with all your mind; and your neighbor as yourself." Romans 3:21-26 is a classic summary of Paul's understanding of justification by faith.

logion. In NT studies, a technical term meaning a succinct "saying" of Jesus (pl. *logia*). It is often used of sayings collected in such hypothetical documents as *Q, which antedate the written *Gospels. *Papias, an early church father (c. A.D. 70-160), is quoted by *Eusebius as maintaining that "Matthew composed the logia *(ta logia)* in the Hebrew tongue and everyone interpreted them as he was able" (Eusebius, *Hist. Eccl.* 3.39.16).

Lord's Supper. *See* Eucharist.

lower criticism. *Textual criticism. The term was developed by J. G. *Eichhorn in contrast with *higher criticism, which critically investigates matters of authorship, date, sources and composition. Neither term is used much in recent scholarship.

Luke-Acts. Luke's two-volume work, the Gospel of Luke and the book of Acts.

Luther, Martin (1483-1546). Sixteenth-century Reformer. Luther, who is credited with launching the Reformation, lectured on the Bible at the University of Wittenberg for many years. His study of Scripture, the influence of *Augustine on his theology, and reading the mystics of his day eventually led to his break with the Roman Church. Luther's "reformed" theology centered on *sola fide* (faith alone), *sola gratia* (grace alone) and *sola Scriptura* (the Bible alone). He is noted in biblical studies for his translation of the Bible into German (completed in 1534). His published biblical studies included his lectures on the Psalms, Romans and Galatians. His *Lectures on Galatians* is considered to be particularly profound theologically.

LXX. *See* Septuagint.

M

M tradition. Gospel material that is uniquely found in Matthew's Gospel. In B. H. Streeter's proposal of the *Four-Source Hypothesis, M signifies material that is unique to Matthew, such as the genealogy and certain events surrounding Jesus' birth (Mt 1—2) as well as certain parables (e.g., 13:44-46; 20:1-16).

Maccabees, Maccabean revolt. The leaders and the Jewish revolt against the Seleucids named after them. In 167 B.C. Mattathias, the father of Judas Maccabeus (Aramaic, "the Hammer"), led a revolt against Antiochus IV Epiphanes. Antiochus had defiled the temple by offering sacrifices to pagan gods (the *abomination of desolation) and had issued an interdiction against several Jewish laws (sabbath observance and circumcision). Judas succeeded his father, who died early in the rebellion, and by 165 B.C. the temple was seized and rededicated with an eight-day celebration (modern Hanukkah). What began as a rebellion to regain religious freedom eventually led to a fight for national independence, which was achieved under John Hyrcanus, the son of Judas's brother Simon, in 135 B.C. The dynasty of Maccabees is also known as the *Hasmoneans (the name of an ancestor of the Maccabees).

magic. The attempt to invoke, control and manipulate supernatural powers (either good or evil) for one's own agenda by using certain formulas or performing certain rituals. Sometimes also referred to as sorcery or witchcraft, magic was a common practice throughout the ancient Near Eastern, Mediterranean and Greco-Roman worlds. The Israelites were warned against such practices (Deut 18:10-11). The NT identifies Simon, a sorcerer in Samaria (Acts 8:9), as well as individuals who practiced magic in Ephesus (19:18-19).

magician. One who engages in *magic.

Magnificat. Mary's song of praise to the Lord. The term is derived from the Latin *Magnificat anima mea Dominum*, "My soul magnifies the Lord," the opening phrase of Mary's song of praise after she and her cousin Elizabeth shared their joy about the birth of Jesus (Lk 1:46). Scholars have observed that the *hymn is modeled after the song of Hannah (1 Sam 2:1-10) and that its language is in the style of the *Septuagint. *See also* Benedictus; Nunc Dimittis.

Major Prophets. Isaiah, Jeremiah and Ezekiel. The distinction between "major" and *"minor" prophets is first found in Latin churches and refers to the size and not the value of the books. *See* Minor Prophets.

majuscule. *See* uncial.

mantic wisdom. A type of *wisdom akin to divination and associated with royal courts and temples in the ancient world. The wise men, or counselors, worked on the principle that the things of the earth and those of the heavens correspond, and that one can learn to interpret "signs" (various phenomena such as entrails, heavenly bodies, and the like) to predict events or plot a course of action. While the Bible prohibits most of these practices (e.g., astrology), Joseph and Daniel are sometimes associated with this type of wisdom because they interpreted dreams for the pharaoh and king respectively.

Manual of Discipline. *See Rule of the Community.*

maranatha. An Aramaic expression *māranā' tā'* transliterated into Greek, meaning "Our Lord, come! (1 Cor 16:22; *Did.* 10.6) or possibly "our Lord has come" (*māran 'ªtā'*). The early Christian context for using this term probably would have been the celebration of the *Eucharist, in which the Lord's presence would be invoked. John uses the term *eschatologically when he ends Revelation with the Greek petition, "Come, Lord Jesus" (*erchou kyrie Iēsou*, 22:20).

Marcion (c. A.D. 100-165). Early Christian heretic. Marcion, an early church leader in Rome, was expelled from the church around A.D. 144 because of his rejection of the OT, his unorthodox views of God and the contradictions that he saw between the OT and the NT. Marcion prefaced his edition of the Scriptures with a series of *Antitheses*, which set out the incompatibility of law and *gospel and the differences between the nature of God in the OT and NT. His list of ten of Paul's letters (in which he calls Ephesians "the epistle to the Laodiceans") is the earliest list known today.

Mark, Secret Gospel of. An *apocryphal *Gospel. The *Secret Gospel of Mark* is a conflated form of Mark's Gospel, known only from a letter reportedly written by *Clement of Alexandria in which he quotes two passages from it (Morton Smith is apparently the only scholar to have seen the manuscript copy of Clement's letter, in 1958 in a Palestinian monastery). Most scholars believe that the Gospel is nothing more than an imitation of the *canonical Gospel of Mark, composed to support certain esoteric initiations.

mashal. Hebrew term often translated "proverb" but covering a variety of literary forms from taunt to *parable. Habakkuk 2:6 exemplifies the diversity of usage: "Shall not everyone taunt [*māšāl*] such people and, with mocking riddles, say about them." *See also* proverb.

Masorah. Marginal notes that were transmitted with the traditional text of the Hebrew Bible. The Hebrew term *māsōrâ* means "tradition," so the term can be used of rules that govern the passing down of the text. *See also* Masoretes; Textus Receptus.

Masoretes. Copyists and scholars who preserved the traditional text of the *Hebrew Bible (the Hebrew term means "traditionalists"). These scholars were responsible for transmitting the consonantal text, compiling the vocalization and accents, and marking other textual notes that help readers and safeguard the integrity of the text. The work of the Masoretes is difficult to date with precision, but they probably began their work as early as the seventh century A.D. The most famous Masoretes were of the Ben Asher family, which was responsible for the oldest *codex known to scholars, the Cairo Codex of the *Prophets, dated A.D. 895. *See also* Masorah; Textus Receptus.

materialist criticism. Also called political criticism, an approach that sees the text as a *physical product* that was produced and kept current through the interests and power of those it benefited. Texts come into existence at particular historical times and in particular socioeconomic settings. The materialist critic seeks to identify those who benefited most from a text, such as the rich and the powerful. A materialist reading focuses more on the human origin of biblical texts and tends to relativize the text's authority. Even a text such as the *Decalogue, materialist critics maintain, has in view the rights of married males who own property and are respected enough in society to give true and false testimony. Materialist criticism is often associated with liberation theologians, who attempt to combine theology with sociopolitical concerns. Issues of class and gender are at the forefront of materialist-critical concerns.

maxim. *See* aphorism; proverb.

Megilloth. The "Festival Books" of the Hebrew Bible (Ruth, Song of Solomon, Ecclesiastes, Lamentations, Esther). *See also* Tanak.

merkabah **mysticism.** A Jewish mysticism centered on the "throne-chariot" (from the Hebrew term *merkābâ*, "chariot") of Ezekiel 1 and Isaiah 6. These visions by Ezekiel and Isaiah, together with the account of creation in Genesis, formed the basis for early Jewish speculation about ascent into heaven and the throne-chariot upon which God sat. In Jewish tradition one rarely finds any indication that the mystic becomes "one" with God, although the mystic could experience an ecstatic transformation while apprehending these divine mysteries. Some see *merkabah* mystical influence in Paul's comments regarding his being caught up into the "third heaven" (cf. 2 Cor 12:2-4). The meaning of *merkabah* mysticism is often extended to include any mystical speculations on the celestial realms.

Merneptah Stela. A *stela commemorating the victory that the Egyptian pharaoh Merneptah (or Merenptah, c. 1213-1203 B.C.) won against the "Sea Peoples." This stela, erected in the pharaoh's temple in Thebes in 1209 B.C., gives us the earliest nonbiblical reference to Israel: "Israel is laid waste; his seed is not." The Merneptah Stela is important for determining the date of the exodus and conquest, though only in the relative sense that by the time of the stela "Israel" was in the land of Canaan. It does not help us determine when Israel left Egypt or the route taken, which are perennial problems for historians.

Mesha Stela. *See* Moabite Stone.

Mesopotamia. The region "between the rivers"—the Euphrates to the west and the Tigris to the east. Historically the region was divided by the Assyrian Empire in the north and the Babylonian Empire in the south, though culturally the inhabitants shared a similar language, similar pantheons of gods and similar laws and stories. The region became important to a large extent because of the alluvium created by the rivers. This rich soil led to farming, which required basic social organization to create a system of canals from the rivers. Once the canals were developed, more sedentary life could flourish. At this point written records of history also emerged. *See also* Akkadian; Fertile Crescent.

messenger formula. A term used by *form critics to label the words "thus says the LORD," which repeatedly occur in prophetic speech to introduce prophetic oracles. The words "thus says" were used of messengers generally in the ancient Near East for oral communication and were adapted by the prophets to indicate the authority and divine origin of the message. For example, each of Amos's *oracles against the nations begins with this formula (1:3, 6, 9, 11, 13; 2:1, 4, 6; cf. Nahum 1:12; Hag 1:2).

Messianic Secret. A term apparently coined by William *Wrede with the publication of his book *The Messianic Secret in the Gospels* (German, 1901). Wrede believed that Mark's theme of silence (see 1:34, 44; 3:11-12; 5:43; 8:27-30) was a theological construct intended to solve a theological dilemma in the early church: if Jesus was the Messiah all along, as the church later affirmed after the resurrection, why did the disciples and his followers not recognize this throughout his ministry? By so arguing, Wrede undermined the views of those who claimed that Mark's *Gospel was the most historically reliable and could be trusted for reconstructing a "life of Jesus." The term, however, has also been used by those who believe that Mark faithfully relates Jesus' actual strategy of concealing his identity.

metaphor. In general usage, an implied comparison in which the characteristics, qualities or actions of one thing are applied to another (e.g., speaking of God as shepherd). A more sophisticated analysis of metaphor yields two elements: the *tenor* is the subject to which the metaphoric word is applied; the *vehicle* is the metaphoric word itself (e.g., "God" is the tenor, and "shepherd" is the vehicle). A further analysis asks how metaphors achieve their purposes, whether by *substitution* (as a decorative way of saying something that could be stated more literally) or by *emotive effect* (its importance is less in what it says and more in the impact it has on the audience) or by *increment* (as a unique cognitive vehicle that allows an author to say a thing that can be said in no other way). Janet Soskice in *Metaphor and Religious Language* (1985) argues that a cautious theological realism best explains how language is used when speaking about God. Thus, for example, to speak of God as father or warrior or in mother imagery is truly to say something about the nature of God, however tentative and inadequate that language may be in saying something comprehensive about God.

metathesis. The transposition ("change of place") of letters, words or phrases during the process of copying manuscripts by hand. In Mark 14:65, for example, *elabon* ("took") appears as *ebalon* ("threw") in some manuscripts. *See also* textual criticism.

midrash. A specific form of Jewish biblical exposition or the genre characterized by this form. The term *midrash* (pl. midrashim) is a form of the Hebrew verb *dāraš*, "to seek, investigate." The term suffers from an overload of meanings. Most simply, it refers to the ancient Jewish commentaries (midrashim) on the Bible that employ a *homiletical approach to interpretation in which stories and parables prevail over propositions. Midrash is thus an interpretive method (anthological and homiletical) of texts that hold authoritative status within Judaism. For example, the *Targumim, the *Talmuds and other compilations of scriptural interpretations that contain midrashic comments (e.g., *Pirqe Aboth) are authoritative texts within Judaism. We also find elements of midrash in the Bible: Chronicles takes stories from Joshua—2 Kings and reworks them with a definite "sermonic" style (*see* inner-biblical exegesis), and Matthew compiles various prophecies to show Jesus as the Messiah whom "Moses, David, and the Prophets" told about.

mimesis. The interpretation of reality in literary texts (from Gk *mimēsis*, "imitation"). Mimesis has to do with a particular style in which an incident is related. For example, in classical antiquity a sublime style was used only for sublime incidents (e.g., tragedy was written in stylized language). Modern realism, by contrast, developed a variety of forms to portray the changing faces of modern life. The Bible often portrays everyday life with a mixture of styles, but in contrast to modern realism it employs *figura,* or *typology, in which events and people across time and even beyond time (heaven) connect with one another within the divine plan. Thus, mimesis refers to how one represents events in a text.

Minor Prophets. The twelve prophetic books (shorter in length than the *Major Prophets), including Hosea, Joel, Amos, Obadiah, Jonal, Micah, Nahum, Habakkuk, Zephaniah, Haggai, Zechariah and Malachi. *See* Book of the Twelve.

minuscule. In textual studies, the term given to small, cursive or "running" letters. This style of writing was used extensively by the ninth to tenth centuries A.D., replacing the earlier *uncial style.

miracle story. A story describing the occurrence of a miracle by Jesus, Paul or another biblical person. The term is also used in a technical sense for such stories in *form-critical analyses of the *Gospels. *See also* aretalogy.

Mishnah. A corpus of Jewish legal material based on rabbinic discussion and interpretation of biblical laws. The Hebrew term *mišnâ* means "study" or "repetition." Before it was codified in the late second century A.D., this material existed in *oral form. In it rabbis sought to apply biblical laws to a new setting, most notably one in which there was no temple and thus no sacrifice. The Mishnah is the focal point of another layer of rabbinic tradition that is enshrined in the *Talmud.

Mithra. An ancient Persian god. Mithraism, the worship of Mithra (as a sun god in its Roman form), spread rapidly throughout the Roman Empire during the first century, not least because it was adopted by many Roman soldiers.

Moabite Stone. A monument commemorating the campaign of the Moabite king Mesha against the Israelite king Omri (cf. 2 Kings 3). The *stela was discovered in 1868 and is dated to approximately 835 B.C. The inscription is written in Moabite, a language nearly identical to the biblical Hebrew of that period. The Moabite Stone gives scholars a source of information regarding the language and history of Israel outside the biblical text, and it mentions Israel's God, *Yahweh.

monolatry. *See* henotheism.

Mowinckel, Sigmund (1884-1965). Scandinavian OT scholar. Mowinckel is best known for his application and extension of the *form-critical method of Herman *Gunkel. In his influential book *The Psalms in Israel's Worship*, Mowinckel refined the classification of the literary forms of the psalms and put forth the hypothesis that the psalms that speak of *Yahweh's kingship were part of *enthronement festivals celebrated each year in the *cult of ancient Israel. The work of Mowinckel (and Gunkel) continues to influence modern critical study of biblical psalms, where interpretation is sought in the literary form (*lament; *hymn) and the cultic life of Israel, not in the historical events found in many of the psalms' superscriptions.

multiple attestation, criterion of. A criterion for determining the authenticity of the sayings of Jesus. The underlying assumption of this criterion is that if similar words and deeds of Jesus are multiply attested in different *Gospel sources (Mark, Q, M, L), they are likely to be authentic. *See also* coherence, criterion of; criteria of authenticity; dissimilarity, criterion of.

Muratorian Canon. A *codex containing a list of twenty-two NT books accepted by the churches at the time it was composed. It is named after L. A. Muratori, who discovered it in 1740. Scholars disagree on whether the list goes back to A.D. 200 or 400.

mystery. In the NT, something that was previously hidden but now has been revealed as part of God's saving activity (from the Greek *mystērion*). The majority of NT occurrences of this word are in the Pauline corpus, where most instances deal directly with the salvation of Gentiles and Paul's apostolic role as a revealer of this mystery. Ephesians 3:3, for example, states: "how the mystery was made known to me by revelation" (see also Rom 16:25; Eph 3:9; Col 1:26-27).

mystery religions. The name given to a number of religious cults of ancient origin and syncretistic tendencies and practices that prevailed from the eighth century B.C. to the fourth century A.D. The term *mystery* comes from the fact that these cults practiced secret initiations. Some of the more popular mystery religions during the Greco-Roman period included the Eleusinian, Dionysiac and Mithraic (*Mithra) mysteries and the mysteries of Isis and Osiris. Scholars have long debated their relationship to the Christian faith because they were very popular during the early centuries A.D. and share some similar practices and vocabulary with Christianity. *See also* history of religions school.

myth. A story, usually relating the actions of supernatural beings, that serves to explain why the world is as it is and to establish the rationale for the rules by which people live in a given society. In classical Greek, myths were simply stories or plots, whether true or false; in modern popular usage, myths are fanciful at best and generally understood as false. *Myth* has become a prominent term for scholars, but it is used in a variety of ways, so care should be taken to understand what sense is being advocated (myths can be, among other things, literary archetypes, widely held fallacies or even realistic, though imagined worlds). The extent to which the Bible can be said to contain myth depends upon the precise signification given to the term. For example, the story of the "sons of God" marrying the "daughters of humans" (Gen 6:1-4) is seen by some as a fanciful story of gods marrying humans, by others as a story of the deep-seated reality of evil in the world and the capacity for humans to participate in that evil, and by still others as a historical allusion to ancient kings exercising the "right of the first night" over women given in marriage. Brevard *Childs argues for the presence of "broken myths" in the Bible (*Myth and Reality in the Old Testament*, 1960), contending that the OT reality of the redemptive activity of God is at variance with myth in the sense that, in myths, reality lies in the processes of nature, not the activity of a transcendent God. Myth may or may not be a derogatory term when used by scholars, but one should be alert to the meaning a particular scholar gives to the term.

Myth and Ritual School. A group of scholars typified by an approach to the OT that seeks to explain a text on the basis of comparative religion, especially the fundamental patterns that underlie the religions of the ancient Near East. The Myth and Ritual School came about through the concerns and writings of British anthropologists but was adopted in particular by Scandinavian scholars of the Uppsala school, who carried the theories further. This approach views the *cult as central in understanding much of the OT, arguing that the practices and perspective of the cult form the basis of religious texts over against specifically doctrinal or even ethical concerns. Thus the rituals of the cult ensured the well-being of the people, and the stories (*myths) recited during these rituals told of the original, usually seasonal, impetus for the ritual. For example, Sigmund *Mowinckel sought to explain various psalms in relation to specific Israelite festivals (New Year; *enthronement; etc.), not just on the basis of their literary forms (*see* form criticism). Scholars of this school maintain that we get a "true picture" of biblical beliefs in the Israelites' rites and festivals in relation to their cultural milieu. *See also* history of religions school.

N

Nag Hammadi Library. A collection of Coptic papyrus documents found near Nag Hammadi, a city in Upper Egypt. This important collection of fifty-two texts in twelve codices (there are fragments of a thirteenth *codex) was discovered in a jar in 1945-1946. The texts are dated to the fourth century but are copies of earlier Greek documents dating to the second and early third centuries. Most of them are *gnostic in nature, and as primary documents they shed significant light on the religious movement known as *Gnosticism.

narrative criticism. An approach to biblical texts that focuses on their narrative features. The narrative critic is concerned with plot and characterization, not with the historical reliability or theology of a passage. For example, *Luke-Acts is the *story* of Jesus and the early church, and while this story assumes that certain events occurred, what is interesting to the narrative critic is the selection and plotting of these events. Even non-narrative books—the prophetic books, for example—have a story substructure: the substructure of Micah is that the *covenant God of Israel will act in history, bringing forth judgment and, ultimately, deliverance to his people. Narrative criticism views story as fundamental to human experience. *See also* implied author; implied reader; literary criticism.

Nebiim. The second part of the Hebrew *canon, the Former and Latter *Prophets (Hebrew *n^ebi'im* means "prophets"). The Former Prophets include Joshua, Judges, 1 and 2 Samuel, 1 and 2 Kings. The Latter Prophets are Isaiah, Jeremiah, Ezekiel and the Twelve (Hosea, Joel, Amos, Obadiah, Jonah, Micah, Nahum, Habakkuk, Zephaniah, Haggai, Zechariah, Malachi). *See also* Tanak.

Nestle, Eberhard (1851-1913). German scholar best known for his critical text of the Greek New Testament, first published in 1898 and now in its twenty-seventh edition.

Nicea, Council of. *See* Council of Nicea.

Nicholas de Lyra (1270-1349). Medieval interpreter of the Bible.

Nicholas studied Hebrew and was well acquainted with the Jewish commentaries, notably those of *Rashi (he would quote Jewish interpretations against those of the early church fathers). His concern for the literal sense over against the *allegorical sense often earn him high marks by some modern commentators, yet he does allow for the "mystical" sense of a passage when it is grounded in the literal. His commentary on Scripture was the first printed.

Noahic covenant. The *covenant God made with Noah (Gen 9). In Jewish thought, since the Noahic covenant was made with the whole of creation and not exclusively with the children of Israel, Gentiles are responsible only to follow the stipulations of this covenant, not the Mosaic covenant. The Noahic covenant is very simple, lacking the complexity and subtlety of the Mosaic and Davidic covenants, yet it still testifies to God's commitment and relationship to the natural and orderly processes of creation (the rainbow becomes the "sign" of the covenant). *See also* Council of Jerusalem.

nomina sacra. Latin for "sacred names." In copying ancient NT manuscripts, sacred names and titles, such as God, Jesus, Christ and Son, were abbreviated or contracted to save space and time (e.g., God: θεός = ΘΣ; Christ: Χριστός = ΧΣ).

Noth, Martin (1902-1968). German OT scholar. Noth is best known for his theory of a *Deuteronomistic History, in which Deuteronomy is not the concluding section of the *Pentateuch but a preface to the history of Israel as told in Joshua, Judges, 1 and 2 Samuel, and 1 and 2 Kings. He also advocated the *amphictyony theory of the twelve-tribe system of Israel.

Novum Testamentum. The Latin title for the NT.

Nunc Dimittis. The Latin title for Simeon's prayer. The title is taken from the first two words of the Latin translation of Simeon's prayer at the time of Jesus' dedication in the temple in Luke 2:29-32: *Nunc dimittis servum tuum Domine* ("Master, now you are dismissing your servant"). It is debated whether this reflects a tradition relating Simeon's words or is an adaptation of an early Jewish *hymn. *See also* Benedictus; Magnificat.

Nuzi Texts. *Akkadian texts found at Nuzi in northern Iraq. These texts (discovered 1925-1941) have played an important role in the comparative study of the OT world of the second millennium B.C. The Nuzi texts comprise more than four thousand *cuneiform documents covering legal matters, social customs and *myths. Some of the practices resemble customs that we find in the *patriarchal narratives and law codes of the *Pentateuch, including inheritance and marriage practices. These texts must be used with caution, however, in any attempt to establish the date of the patriarchs, since the laws and customs the texts relate were part of the general ancient Near Eastern milieu that extended even into the first millennium in some form.

O

oikoumenē. Greek word used for the world, the inhabited earth and humankind. The term stands behind the English *ecumenism*—the desire to embrace and unify the inhabited world or, more specifically, all believers in Jesus Christ (Jn 17:21; 1 Cor 12:12-20; Eph 4:4-6).

omega. *See* alpha and omega.

oracles against the nations. Divine messages given to a prophet to speak judgment against a foreign nation. For example, the book of Amos begins with a series of judgments against the nations that surround Israel and Judah (Amos 1:3—2:3; cf. Is 13—23; Jer 46—51). These oracles encouraged and comforted Judah and testified to God's sovereignty: "But as for you, have no fear, my servant Jacob . . . for I am going to save you from far away" (Jer 46:27). Note, however, that Amos ended his oracles against the nations with extended and pointed words against both Judah and Israel (Amos 2:4-11). Indeed, Judah and Israel were even more culpable than other nations since they had been delivered from Egypt by God and given the *Torah to live by (Amos 2:4, 10).

oral tradition. Stories, poems, teachings, sayings, and the like that are passed down orally rather than in written form. In antiquity, orality was the predominant tool for disseminating and preserving culture. Even into the *Hellenistic period, when written texts increased significantly, the hearing of a text was highly regarded (e.g., Rom 10:17). The use of mnemonic (memory) devices, rhetorical expressions and formulaic structures facilitated the passing down of these traditions and the preservation of their integrity, though freedom was also exercised to adapt and highlight elements. Oral tradition has an immediacy that written texts do not, since the speaker and audience can respond to one another directly.

Origen (c. 185-254). Early church father. Origen was one of the earliest and most influential members of the *Alexandrian school. He was born in Egypt and studied under *Clement of Alexandria. Origin eventually established a school in Caesarea, where he preached and wrote voluminously, though only fragments of his works are extant. As a biblical scholar he is most famous for his work as a *textual critic, in which he arranged various translations of Scripture side by side in columns in a work known as the *Hexapla. As a commentator and theologian, he excelled in the *allegorical interpretation of Scripture. Book 4 of his *De Principiis* deals with *hermeneutics, explaining the literal, moral and allegorical uses of Scripture.

ossuary. A casket carved from limestone or wood used for holding the bones (Latin *ossurarius)* of the dead. Some of these caskets were inscribed or decorated, thus providing clues to beliefs about death and life beyond death. Ossuaries were used for secondary burials, after the flesh had decayed in a primary tomb. The custom prevailed from the Iron Age (the time of the monarchy in Israel) into the NT period.

ostraca. Fragments of pottery recycled for writing notes, lists and even brief hymns or religious maxims. These fragments broaden our understanding of ancient Hebrew *paleography, grammar and syntax, and shed light on the society in which they are found. For example, the Lachish letters are ostraca that give scholars a glimpse of the state of the language and the state of the city of Lachish just prior to its destruction by Nebuchadnezzar in 586 B.C.

Oxyrhynchus papyri. A collection of thousands of ancient *papyrus fragments of the OT and NT as well as *apocryphal and *pseudepigraphal literature. The papyri were discovered by A. S. Hunt and B. P. Grenfell at Oxyrhynchus (modern Behnesa) in Upper Egypt in 1897 and 1907. The fragments date from the second to seventh centuries A.D. and are written in Greek, Latin, Egyptian, Coptic, Hebrew and Syriac.

P

paleography. The study of the history and development of ancient writing. Paleography is used to decipher and date ancient texts and is helpful in *textual criticism for establishing the time and origin of texts.

Palestinian Christians. *See* Jewish Christians.

Palestinian Judaism. The type of Judaism located within the borders of Palestine as it developed between roughly 200 B.C. and A.D. 200. Recent studies in Judaism now speak of "Judaisms" rather than Judaism and realize that Jews in Palestine were not insulated from *Hellenistic ideas. *See also* Jewish Christians.

pantheism. The belief that God and the creation are essentially identical. The Bible portrays God as Creator, and thus it explicitly denies pantheism, since God is distinct from creation (Gen 1).

Papias. An early church father (c. A.D. 70-160), bishop of Hierapolis in Phrygia. He is remembered for his statements that Mark was Peter's "interpreter" *(hermēneutēs)* and that Matthew composed "the logia" in the Hebrew tongue. *See* logion.

papyrus. A tall, aquatic reed that grows in the Nile Delta of Egypt and was made into a writing material of the same name. Papyrus was the main writing surface throughout the Mediterranean world from the fourth century B.C. to the seventh century A.D. The earliest NT Greek manuscripts were written on papyrus. The English word *paper* is derived from the Greek *papyros* and the Latin *papyrus.*

parable. A common literary form found in the OT (Heb *māšāl)* and the NT (Gk *parabolē).* Parables are short, simple stories designed to communicate a spiritual truth or a moral lesson by using examples or making comparisons from everyday life, as in Jesus' parables in the *Gospels. In the OT, *mashal* also covers a broad range of meanings, such as a proverb, riddle, allegory and simile. *See also* proverb.

paradigm. In biblical studies, the term refers either to a model or to a brief narrative. Abraham, for example, is portrayed as a model (paradigm) of faith since he followed God's call without question or hesitation (cf. Gen 12; 22). In *Gospel studies the term refers to the brief stories told by Jesus to pronounce a principle or model of action. Scholars also use the phrase "paradigm shift" to indicate a change of models or perspectives. For example, a paradigm shift has occurred in biblical studies from older forms of *literary criticism (e.g., *source criticism) to newer forms (e.g., *narrative or even *feminist criticism). *See also* apophthegm; pronouncement story.

paradosis. Customs and beliefs that are handed down (Gk *paradosis,* "tradition"), such as the "traditions of the elders" referred to in the *Gospels (Mt 15:2-3; Mk 7:5, 13) or the "human tradition" that Paul contrasts with a revelation from Christ (Col 2:8). Paul valued Christian traditions that he "received" *(paralambanō)* from his early Christian predecessors and in turn "delivered" *(paradidōmi)* to his congregations (1 Cor 11:23-25; 15:3-4).

paraenesis. A technical term referring to various kinds of exhortations or admonitions. In NT studies, the term usually applies to the moral/ethical exhortations given to believers. On a number of occasions, Paul simply refers to instructions or teaching that he has passed on without any indication of its content (1 Cor 11:2; Phil 4:9; Col 2:6-7; 1 Thess 4:2; 2 Thess 2:15; 3:6). But in other places there are rather lengthy paraenetic sections according to the needs of the congregation. In OT studies it is used of the sermonic approach of Chronicles and the prophetic oracles.

parallelism. The characteristic of parallel lines in Hebrew poetry. Parallelism has the effect of saying the "same in the other" (C. S. Lewis) as a thought or an image in the initial line is taken up in the subsequent line(s). In the eighteenth century Robert Lowth identified three forms of parallelism: synonymous, where the second line reproduces the first; antithetical, where the second line is in contrast to the first; and synthetic, where the second line carries the thought of the first forward. Hebrew poetry is deceptively simple to translate because of this parallelistic feature, yet the various ways of balancing one line with another can work on the level of sound, form and even grammatical structures. Recent studies have focused more on the subtlety of balancing that takes place between the lines and the necessity of taking into consideration all the linguistic features, not just the thought that is paralleled. For example, Job 5:14 reads:

> They meet with darkness in the daytime,
> And grope at noonday as in the night.

"Daytime" and "night" are a common contrasting word pair, and here they occupy the same position in the Hebrew (first, not last, as in the translation above). However, the other word pairs—"daytime" and "noonday," "darkness" and "night"—occupy opposite positions in the lines but are similar in meaning (the verbs actually occupy the middle position in each line, and each line is comprised of only three Hebrew words). The poem begins with "daytime" and ends with "noonday" but in between lie "darkness" and "night." Thus the poem is very tightly and artfully constructed around similar and contrasting images that parallel one another.

parataxis. Clauses or phrases linked together without subordinate relationships. Parataxis is a characteristic feature of Hebrew narrative, in which actions are linked with a simple "and" (Heb *wāw*). For example, Jonah 1:3 literally reads: "And Jonah arose . . . and he went down . . . and he found . . . and he gave . . . and he entered." The same feature may be observed in the Gospel of Mark, which employs a *kai* parataxis (e.g., Mk 14:37). Parataxis is also used to describe the narrative style Mark employs in which *pericopes are juxtaposed side by side without immediately apparent connections, though careful reading can discern them.

parchment. Also called vellum; the skin of goats, sheep or other animals specially prepared for use as a writing surface. Parchment was used as early as the second century B.C. The most complete extant manuscripts of the NT were written on vellum.

Parousia. A transliteration of the Greek *parousia*, meaning "coming, arrival" and typically referring to the second coming and presence (*pareimi*) of Christ at the end of time (1 Cor 16:22; Rev 22:7, 12, 20). *See also* eschatology.

Passion Narrative. The *Gospel accounts of the events surrounding Jesus' suffering and death (i.e., "passion"). The Passion Narrative begins with the Jewish plot against Jesus' life during the Feast of Unleavened Bread and ends with his burial (Mt 26—27; Mk 14—15; Lk 22—23). Many *form critics suggest that "passion narratives" were the first written accounts of Jesus' life.

Pastoral Epistles. A collective term for 1 and 2 Timothy and Titus. Since the eighteenth century these letters have been called Pastoral Epistles (or Letters) because of the "pastoral" nature of the advice given to Timothy and Titus, both of whom were leaders in Pauline churches and were dealing with such issues as leadership, church order, false teaching and the moral conduct of believers.

patriarchal history. The stories in Genesis 12—50 that recount the lives of the patriarchs and matriarchs of Israel. These stories might be better termed "narratives" rather than "history," since so many of the events involve personal experiences of God and family life rather than "political" events that would be told in the annals of the surrounding peoples.

patristic era. The time of the "church fathers," roughly from Clement of Rome to *Bede (c. 100-750 A.D.). The writings of these theologians have long been considered authoritative by the church. It was not until the Reformation, and especially the rise of critical studies in the eighteenth century, that their writings were seriously challenged. Patristic interpretation is characterized by seeing Scripture as a person with a body and soul. The "body" is the words of the text itself, the "literal sense" (*sensus literalis), and the "soul" is the "spiritual sense" of the words, the moral and mystical senses (*sensus plenior).

Pauline homologoumena. Letters of Paul uniformly acknowledged as Scripture in the early centuries of the church. Homologoumena is a form of the Greek word homologeō, "to confess, profess." *Eusebius used the term *homologoumena for all the NT books that he considered to be acknowledged as Scripture by the church of his day. The term sometimes appears in discussions of the NT *canon.

Pauline school. A hypothetical group of associates and followers of Paul. Proponents of the *deutero-Pauline hypothesis suggest that during Paul's lifetime—and even after his death—some of his closest coworkers (e.g., Luke, Timothy, Tychicus, Onesimus) may have formed some type of theological school in which Paul's theology and legacy would have been discussed at great length. Ephesus is often proposed as the most likely location because Paul spent three years teaching there (Acts 19:8-10; 20:31), and it is the city where Timothy was working when 1 and 2 Timothy were written.

Paulinism. An expression or theological formulation characteristic of Paul.

Paulinist. A person who continued Paul's legacy. Books believed to be *deutero-Pauline are often said to have been written by a

Paulinist, someone familiar with Paul's theology and writings (*Paulinism) and thus standing within the Pauline heritage. *See also* Pauline school.

pax Romana. Literally, "Roman peace." The *pax Romana* describes the peaceful political conditions in the Roman Empire from the time of Caesar Augustus to the middle of the second century A.D.

Pentateuch. The first five books of the Bible: Genesis, Exodus, Leviticus, Numbers and Deuteronomy. *See also* Torah and Tanak.

pericope. A technical term for a short section or literary unit that has integrity even when "cut off" or "cut out" (Gk *perikoptō*) from a longer narrative. Frequently a pericope will be the focus of *exegesis. In some cases it refers to the basic units of the *Gospels that relate a saying or deed of Jesus and probably circulated separately in the early church before the Evangelists incorporated them into their larger narratives.

peshat. The Hebrew term for the "plain" meaning of a passage. *Peshat* is in contrast to *derash*, the homiletical meaning. *Peshat* and *derash* roughly correspond to the literal and spiritual senses of Scripture in Christian interpretation. *Peshat* was developed especially by the great medieval Jewish commentator *Rashi, who also influenced subsequent Christian interpretation of the Bible. *Peshat* and *derash*, though different in style and content, were often employed side by side and should not be thought of as opposites but rather as having different purposes in the task of interpretation. *See also sensus literalis; sensus plenior.*

pesher. From the Hebrew word meaning "interpretation," a style of commentary found especially in the *Dead Sea Scrolls, in which a verse of Scripture is interpreted with reference to the interpreter's own time and situation, which is usually seen as the last days. For example, the commentary on Habakkuk 1:4 found at Qumran focuses on the Wicked Priest and the Teacher of Righteousness, two prominent figures in the community. We also find examples of pesher exegesis in the NT. For example, in Acts 2:16-20 Peter says that what was happening with the miraculous "speaking in tongues" was what Joel had spoken about centuries before (Joel 2:28-32; see also Acts 4:11 = Ps 118:22; Eph 5:31 = Gen 2:24).

Peshitta. The Syriac translation of the Bible (literally, "Simple Version"). The Peshitta was heavily influenced by the *Septuagint and the *Targumim. The date of the Peshitta could be as early as the second century A.D., though it seems likely that the translation extended over a period of time and was carried out by various translators. However, the influences from the Septuagint and Targums complicate the fixing of a date. Disagreements continue as to whether the translators were Jewish or Christian. Since the text reflects a Hebrew original very close to the *Masoretic Text, the Peshitta contributes as much to our understanding of how a passage was understood by this community as it does to our knowledge of the textual transmission of the Bible. *See also* textual criticism.

Philo of Alexandria (c. 20 B.C.—50 A.D.). A Hellenistic Jewish philosopher, statesman, exegete and contemporary of Jesus and Paul. Philo's statesmanship was exhibited in his leading of a delegation to Rome to complain about riots against the *Hellenistic-Jewish community in Alexandria. The delegation met with some success. His importance for biblical studies lies in his many philosophical writings, which include commentaries on Genesis and Exodus in particular. Philo's use of the *allegorical method of interpretation was highly influential on Christian interpreters (e.g., *Clement of Alexandria, *Origen and *Augustine). His commentaries are also important because he preserves interpretations of his predecessors, though he does not specify who he is drawing upon.

Pirqe Aboth. A collection of maxims from the *Mishnah highlighting the wit and wisdom of the sages (the Hebrew means "sayings/ethics of the fathers"). It also traces a chain of authority from Moses to the prophets, and from the prophets to the men of the Great *Synagogue. The book was popular reading on the Sabbath and is used by Jews today for general instruction. One famous saying is attributed to *Hillel, a first-century rabbi: "If I'm not for myself, who is for me? And when I am for myself, what am I? And if not now, when?"

Platonism. A system of philosophy based on the work of the Athenian philosopher Plato. The philosophical movement called Platonism actually begins with the Academy that Plato established in 387 B.C. and with the pupils that succeeded him after his death in 347 B.C. Although Platonism includes doctrines of metaphysics, logic and ethics, its influence on Western thought includes the concept of "forms" and immortality as well. Plato taught that anything created is an imperfect copy of a transcendent and eternal form, the highest being the form of "the Good." Only after the soul is released from its body at death is it able to contemplate truth in its purest form.

plērōma. A Greek term translated as "fullness" or "completeness." It is used in the NT to refer to the fullness of time, the right time (Gal 4:4; Eph 1:10), the "full inclusion" of the Jews (Rom 11:12) and Gentiles (Rom 11:25), the totality of God's and Christ's being (Eph 3:19; 4:13; Col 1:19; 2:9), as well as the church (Eph 1:23). Some scholars believe that it was a technical term in *gnostic Christianity.

Pliny the Younger (c. A.D. 61/62-113). An administrator of the Roman province of Bithynia during the rule of the emperor Trajan (A.D. 98-117). His correspondence with Trajan is significant for NT studies because he describes believers in his area as a kind of a superstitious cult that regularly met for worship (*Ep.* 10.96).

preexistence. In NT christology, the idea that Christ had a divine existence prior to his incarnation. In some Jewish traditions, we find the belief that divine wisdom was active prior to creation (Job 28:20-27; Prov 8:22-31). In Greek *Platonic philosophy we encounter the idea that the soul existed prior to its bodily habitation. In NT studies and theology, preexistence usually refers to the belief that the Son of God, the second person of the Trinity, existed eternally in heaven with God the Father prior to his incarnation as Jesus of Nazareth. Although the word *preexistence* does not occur in the NT, the concept is deduced from a number of texts (Jn 1:1, 14; 3:13; 6:38, 62; 10:30; 1 Cor 8:6; Phil 2:6; Col 1:15; Heb 1:1-2).

prescript. The opening of a letter, comprising the name of the sender and of the addressee as well as a greeting. Many of Paul's letters begin this way, as, for example, Colossians 1:1-2: "Paul, an apostle of Christ Jesus by the will of God, and Timothy our brother, to the saints and faithful brothers and sisters in Christ in Colossae: Grace to you and peace from God our Father."

priestly blessing. Text found in Numbers 6:24-26 where the Lord instructs Moses (and the priests) to bless the people.

Priestly source. According to the *Documentary Hypothesis, the designation of the *pentateuchal source that reflects the traditions and theological perspective of the priests. Designated P, this source begins with the creation of the world (Gen 1) and extends into Joshua. Dating the Priestly source has been difficult, and in recent years some scholars have posited an H (Holiness) source, which is claimed to be responsible for further development of the priestly concerns, thus accounting for the widely divergent views on the date for P as eighth or sixth century. Characteristic of P is the belief in a single God unopposed by any other divine or demonic powers. Any "threat" to God comes from humans who, given free will, defy God through moral and ritual sins. This threat to holiness can even drive God from his temple. In the symbolic system of holiness, Israel chooses life or death and thereby chooses for or against God. Reparation is possible through the ritual system, thus restoring one to the community and the community to God. *See also* source criticism.

primeval history. The stories told in Genesis 1—11 that recount the origins and primordial history of humankind—creation, Noah and the tower of Babel—leading up to the stories of the *patriarchs.

Promised Land. The land of *Canaan. Used especially in Jewish thought to emphasize the link with the divine promises to the patriarchs (see Gen 12:1).

pronouncement story. In *form criticism of the *Gospels, the name given by Vincent Taylor to brief stories or narratives told by Jesus for the sake of making a "pronouncement" of some kind. A good example is the question about paying taxes to Caesar (Mk 12:13-17), where the story frames the pronouncement: "Give to the emperor the things that are the emperor's, and to God the things that are God's" (12:17).

Prophets, Former and Latter. The second section of the Hebrew *canon, the *Nebiim. *See also* Tanak.

proselyte. A person who becomes a convert to another religious faith and a member of that community. Many OT laws recognize the rights and privileges of "strangers" or "resident aliens" within Judaism, although it is not clear whether such groups were regarded as "full" or "complete" Jews. Later rabbinic material (*Mishnah) describes a conversion process that required study of the law, circumcision for males, baptism by immersion, and sacrifice. There are several references to proselytes *(prosēlytos)* in the NT (see Acts 2:11; 6:5; 13:43). Proselytes should be distinguished from the so-called Gentile God-fearers *(theosebēs)* who were attracted to Judaism (probably because of its monotheism and high ethical standards) but did not become full adherents to Jewish faith and life (see "worshipper of God," Acts 16:14; 18:7). Jewish and pagan converts to Christianity were required to believe in Jesus Christ and to be baptized "in the name of Jesus Christ" (Acts 2:38).

protoevangelium. The first, or earliest, declaration of the *gospel (Gk *prōtos,* "first," + *euangelion,* "gospel") in Genesis 3:15, where God rebukes the serpent by predicting that Eve's offspring will crush the devil's offspring. Since the second century this verse has traditionally been seen as the first glimmer of the gospel that God's purpose in creation will be fulfilled in spite of the fall of humanity.

proto-Luke. In the *Four-Source Hypothesis proposed by B. H. Streeter, proto-Luke is a hypothetical document that Streeter believed was composed of *Q and *L material only, and that existed prior to our current version of Luke's Gospel.

proto-Matthew. A hypothetical version of Matthew that some scholars think existed prior to our *canonical Gospel of Matthew. It is not necessarily identified as the supposed Aramaic original lying behind our Greek version.

provenance. The place of origin of a document. For example, some scholars claim a Palestinian or Syrian provenance for the Fourth *Gospel; others opt for Asia Minor.

proverb. A brief, popular saying summarizing a piece of wisdom about common human experiences: "A penny saved is a penny earned." Proverbs often seem commonplace and even boring, but if one begins to ponder these sayings as "little poems" and picture the "story" that is portrayed in the proverb, they can be quite powerful and enlightening. The biblical proverbs—sometimes referred to as epigrams or *aphorisms, since they are often polished and pointed (witty or satirical)—are intended as instructions on the "art of living well" and invite the reader to look at the world from the distinctive view of faith, the "fear of the Lord." For example, Proverbs 26:9 reads: "Like a thornbush brandished by the hand of a drunkard is a proverb in the mouth of a fool." What is pictured is a swashbuckling drunk wielding a thornbush for a sword—such is a wise saying in the hands of a fool! Proverbs require both skill and discernment to plumb the art of living well (cf. Prov 1:2-7 and 1—9 generally). In the NT, note Matthew 6:21 ("For where your treasure is, there your heart will be also") and 26:52 ("For all who take the sword will perish by the sword"). *See also mashal;* parallelism.

Psalter. The entire collection of the Psalms. The Psalter is divided into five books: 1-41 (Book I); 42-72 (Book II); 73-89 (Book III); 90-106 (Book IV); and 107-150 (Book V).

Pseudepigrapha. A collection of ancient Jewish and *Hellenistic writings that were written during the intertestamental period but are not part of the *canonical OT or the *Apocrypha (see James Charlesworth, ed., *The Old Testament Pseudepigrapha,* 2 vols.). This collection includes various types of literature, some of it attributed to biblical persons, such as Enoch, Ezra, Baruch, Elijah, Abraham, Isaac and Jacob, but in reality these names are pseudonyms.

pseudonymous. A false (Gk *pseudos*) claim of authorship for a literary work, in Jewish literature usually a great figure of the distant past. The Wisdom of Solomon purports to be written by Solomon, but evidence suggests that a Greek-speaking Jew wrote it many centuries after Solomon. The various books of *Enoch* claim to be written by the ancient and enigmatic figure by that name (Gen 5:21-24). The practice of writing pseudonymously was common in antiquity, and many scholars argue that certain NT books (e.g., Ephesians) are pseudonymous. *See also* deutero-Pauline.

Q

Q source. A hypothetical document consisting of a collection of Jesus' sayings. Q is an abbreviation of the German word *Quelle,* "source." In the *Two-Source Hypothesis of the *Synoptic problem, Q accounts for sayings of Jesus that are common to Matthew and Luke but are not found in Mark (approximately 230 verses). There is no universal scholarly agreement on Q's origin, date, *provenance or theological perspective.

qal wahomer. A rule of *rabbinic interpretation stating that what is true in a less-important case is even truer in a more-important case. This is a rabbinic formulation of the Latin dictum *a minori ad maius,* "from the lesser to the greater."

qinah. The Hebrew term for "lament," used of the 3:2 meter sometimes found in biblical laments. In these *laments the first of the
parallel lines (*see* parallelism) is longer, having three stresses,
while the second line has only two. This pattern gives the lines a
"limping" feeling. A problem arises in identifying this metrical
pattern with laments: we also find the *qinah* pattern in poetic lines
that are not laments, while some laments actually have a 3:3 pattern rather than the more common 3:2. Many scholars question the
existence of meter in Hebrew poetry because of the many problems and divergencies of metrical identification.

Qoheleth. Hebrew term meaning "preacher" (also spelled Koheleth), and the Hebrew name for the book of Ecclesiastes.

Quest of the Historical Jesus. The scholarly quest to discover the real,
historical figure of Jesus who stands behind the *Gospel accounts.
The term is taken from the English title of Albert *Schweitzer's famous book, *The Quest of the Historical Jesus.* The Quest of the Historical Jesus has come to refer to various and ongoing attempts to
write a historically reliable account of Jesus. The story of this scholarly pursuit has even been labeled by periods: the Old Quest
(1778—1900); the "No Quest" (1900—1940); the New Quest
(1940—1980); and the Third Quest (1980—present). This last
Quest, coined by N. T. Wright, seeks to understand Jesus primarily
within the context of first-century Jewish culture and tends to rely
less on the *criteria of authenticity (particularly the criterion of
*dissimilarity) than on seeing Jesus as a credible figure within first-
century *Palestinian Judaism.

Qumran. A site on the northwest shore of the Dead Sea whose ruins
are associated with the scrolls discovered there in 1947 by shepherds looking for their sheep. The ancient community that lived at
Qumran produced many of the *Dead Sea Scrolls. *See also* Essenes.

R

rabbinic Judaism. The Jewish sages ("rabbis" = "teachers") represented in the *Mishnah, *Talmuds and *midrashic traditions that
were collected and codified in the early centuries of the Christian
era, as well as the beliefs and practices that were defined by these
writings. The origins of these rabbis may date to the Persian period

(fifth-century B.C.) with the rise of the *sopherim* (scribes), but their authoritative status did not fully emerge until the destruction of Jerusalem in the first-century A.D. and the radical reorientation of Jewish life that followed from the absence of temple worship and a priestly and political hierarchy.

Rad, Gerhard von (1901-1971). German OT scholar. Von Rad's ability to combine searching scholarship, vibrant faith and beautiful prose made him one of the most widely read and respected OT theologians of the twentieth century. He is best known for his commentary on *Genesis* and his two-volume *Old Testament Theology*, in which he emphasized the vitality of dissimilar traditions to be heard and actualized as *Yahweh's word for each new generation. Unlike Walther *Eichrodt, von Rad shaped his OT theology around the history of traditions rather than a central theme. The importance of the *cult in shaping beliefs and of confessional statements in transmitting faith were primary concerns for von Rad.

Ras Shamra Texts. *See* Ugarit.

Rashi (1040-1105). Rabbi Solomon ben Isaac (Rashi) is the most famous Jewish interpreter of the Bible. His judicious comments and terse style won him renown among Christian commentators. He greatly influenced all subsequent translators of the Bible. His commentary on the *Torah was the first to be printed in Hebrew (1475).

reader-response criticism. A literary approach to the text that turns from an author to the reader to fill in the gaps in a text. In its more radical form, this approach regards the "meaning" not in the structure and words of the text but in the meeting point of the reader and the text. Hence, in this approach, the reader is often the "creator" of the meaning since in the act of reading, readers make what they will of what they read. For example, a reader might find support for a vegetarian lifestyle in the initial chapters of Job, where domestic animals play an important role in the agricultural economy of Job, but not explicitly for consumption. The book is not advocating vegetarianism, but readers with those concerns could find support for their position. The reader's interests and concerns become the focal point of interpretation, more so than the author's intent or purposes. *See also* deconstruction.

realized eschatology. The idea that the kingdom of God in Jesus teaching is not future but "realized" in the person and mission

Jesus. The term is attributed to C. H. *Dodd, who developed this understanding particularly in his scholarly work on the *parables. Most interpreters have criticized Dodd's position as too extreme, arguing that although the kingdom of God is present in the life and ministry of Jesus, he nevertheless pointed to a future and final consummation of the kingdom; in other words, the kingdom is both "already and not yet." *See also* eschatology; Parousia.

recension. A revision of an earlier text or document. The term is used especially in OT and NT *textual criticism but occasionally by literary critics to speak of stages in the transmission of a text. Technically speaking, all manuscripts are recensions of the original autographs.

redaction criticism. An approach to a text that seeks to show how authors or editors have selected, shaped and framed sources in composing their work. This approach generally focuses on larger literary units rather than individual verses and often sees the editors of the biblical books as compilers rather than authors in their own rights. In the case of the *Gospels, redaction criticism can be very helpful in showing, for example, how Matthew used Mark and what purpose he had in mind, since we can place the two texts side by side and use Luke as a further point of comparison. Redaction criticism also seeks to show the intentions and viewpoints of books or even a series of books (e.g., *Luke-Acts; *Deuteronomistic History). *See also* tendency criticism.

redactor. The person who edits, revises or shapes literary sources in the composition of a literary work. *See also* redaction criticism.

Redaktionsgeschichte. See redaction criticism.

Reimarus, Hermann Samuel (1694-1768). German Enlightenment scholar. Reimarus was credited by Albert *Schweitzer with initiating the *Quest of the Historical Jesus. Reimarus embraced English Deism and wrote many stinging rationalistic attacks on orthodoxy and the Christian faith. Most of his manuscripts remained unpublished until Gotthold E. Lessing collected and published them as *The Wolfenbüttel Fragments.*

Religionsgeschichtliche Schule. See history of religions school.

remnant. A remainder of righteous people of God who survive judgment or catastrophe. Remnant is a key motif that runs throughout the OT and NT and is found in extrabiblical Jewish literature as well as in ancient Near Eastern literature. The theme can refer to preservation of life from mortal threats (e.g., fire or famine), preservation of the faithful in the midst of apostasy (1 Kings 19:14-18; Rom 11:1-6) and God's salvation of the true people of God even in the face of fears, threats and conflict. Even when God judges Israel, he saves a remnant (Is 10:20-21; Zeph 3:12-13), which is the basis for hope.

rhetorical criticism. An approach to the biblical text that concerns itself with the way language is used in a text to persuade its audience. Style, structure and figures of speech have an affect on the audience or reader of a text, and the rhetorical critic focuses on how this "rhetoric" works rather than focusing on the historical setting of a story or poem. In the OT, this approach is successful in stories where a *Leitwort* or *Leitmotiv* ("lead-word, "lead-theme") recurs throughout the story and is used in various ways (e.g., the term "brother" occurs seven times in the short passage concerning Cain and Abel to highlight the disturbing enmity of these two). It is also particularly helpful in poetry, where the conscious and unconscious selection of words and images—and the rejection of alternate words and images—creates an impression on the reader. For example, Micah 2:6-11 uses various forms of the word *drip* to entrap those who scoff at the prophet and accuse him of dripping/ prophesying: these scoffers who prophesy of wine will "drip" (words) for the people (Mic 2:11). In NT studies, a number of scholars have attempted to interpret the NT letters according to ancient rhetorical categories. These usually include: (1) introduction *(exordium)*; (2) narration *(narratio)*; (3) proposition *(propositio)*; (4) confirmation *(probatio)*; (5) refutation *(refutatio)*; and (6) conclusion *(peroratio)*. The rhetorical critic focuses on the effect the words in a passage have on an audience, how the passage was intended to persuade its audience to a particular point of view.

Rule of the Community. A document that records the beliefs and rules of the community at *Qumran. The *Rule of the Community* (IQS), formerly called the *Manual of Discipline,* is one of the best-known documents of the *Dead Sea Scrolls and is a valuable source for understanding the belief system of one of several Jewish sects of the NT period.

S

Sachkritik, Sachexegese. Content or subject criticism. Both terms derive from the German noun *Sache,* meaning "thing, object, or subject matter." In English the terms usually are translated as "content criticism" and "theological exegesis." In this approach, the interpretation or exegesis of a text is determined by an understanding of the text's real intention or inner logic *(Sache).* Scholars have noted that this process of interpretation creates a hermeneutical circle in which the parts of the text are interpreted in light of the whole, and the whole in light of the parts. A problem arises, however, when scholars dismiss aspects of a text that are determined to be contrary to the true intention of the text.

saga. A genre of narrative that is episodic and focuses on family history or a past hero rather than on political history. Saga is derived from *oral tradition and has little background description but tells the story largely in terms of the characters' actions. The *patriarchal narratives (Gen 12—36) are an example of sagas, or family-stories. *See* legend; etiology.

salvation history. Redemptive history; God's plan of salvation in history. Salvation history is the English translation of the German term *Heilsgeschichte,* which refers not to a methodology but to a theological principle of seeing Scripture as the story of God's ongoing redemptive work in history. It differs, for example, from seeing Scripture as a series prooftexts for constructing a doctrine or attempting to critically discern an "actual" history of "real" events (*Historie)* behind salvation history. *See also* Biblical Theology Movement; Cullmann, Oscar (1902-1999).

Samaritan Pentateuch. A form of the *Pentateuch developed roughly 100 B.C. by the Samaritan community. The Samaritans (who broke with Jews some time prior to the NT period) never accepted the *Prophets and *Writings as Scripture in the same way that the Jews did. Thousands of differences exist between the Samaritan Pentateuch and the Jewish Pentateuch, but most of these are matters of spelling and grammar. The relationship between the two texts is debated and includes questions of how the Hebrew text was transmitted and the complex relationship between the various "Judaisms" of the NT period. Interestingly, the "text type" of the Samaritan Pentateuch has been found among the biblical manuscripts discovered at *Qumran. *See also* textual criticism.

Sanhedrin. A council or assembly (Gk, *synēdrion*) of Jewish leaders. Although the Gospels and Acts use this and other terms to designate various types of councils and judicial courts (see Mt 5:22, 26, 59; Mk 13:9; 14:55; 15:1; Lk 22:66; Acts 5:21), only the tractate "Sanhedrin" in the *Mishnah refers to "the Great Sanhedrin," a body of seventy-one members responsible for final decisions in legal disputes.

Schleiermacher, Friedrich Daniel Ernst (1768-1834). A German scholar frequently referred to as the father of modern or liberal theology (*The Christian Faith*, 1821-1822; 2d ed., 1830-1831). Schleiermacher sought to encourage people who had rejected religion on rational grounds to embrace a mystical and psychological appreciation of God through experience. He is criticized for reducing religion to a subjective "feeling of dependency."

Schweitzer, Albert (1875-1965). Philosopher, theologian, physician, musician and biblical scholar known for his epoch-making book *The Quest of the Historical Jesus* (German *Von Reimarus zu Wrede: Eine Geschichte der Leben-Jesu Forschung* ["From Reimarus to Wrede: A History of the Life of Jesus Research," 1906]), and his medical missionary work in Lambaréné (Gabon). Schweitzer claimed that Jesus was a mistaken *apocalyptic prophet who felt chosen by God to usher in the end of history. However, according to Schweitzer, Jesus failed in this mission and died a disillusioned martyr.

Second Isaiah. Isaiah 40—55, believed by many scholars to be from a different author than Isaiah 1—39 (First Isaiah) and 56—66 (Third or Trito-Isaiah). It is also called Deutero-Isaiah. The style, themes and setting of these chapters differ from the preceding and following chapters and suggest to critical scholars that they were written during the *Babylonian exile (587-537 B.C.), well after the time period of the historical prophet Isaiah in the eighth century B.C. *See also* First Isaiah; Isaiah, multiple authorship of; Third Isaiah.

Second Temple Judaism. The period of Jewish history and literature from the time the second temple was completed around 516 B.C. to the fall of Jerusalem and destruction of Herod's temple by the Romans in A.D. 70. In current scholarly work it is gradually replacing the more common term "Intertestamental Period."

sectarian Judaism. Ideas or movements within Judaism that deviat from the norm (Latin *secta*, "party, faction"). In the NT, "sect" (Gk *hairesis*) is used to describe the Pharisees (Acts 15:5; 26:5), Sadducees (5:17) and the early Christians (24:5, 14; 28:22). The community at *Qumran is sometimes referred to as another form of sectarian Judaism. Today, most scholars recognize that first-century *Palestinian Judaism was pluralistic and that there was no monolithic, normative Judaism. For this reason, when dealing with this period it is preferable to speak of Judaisms or types of Judaism rather than Judaism.

Semites. Latinized name for the sons of "Shem" and the languages they spoke (cf. Gen 10:21-31). Semitic languages are separated into three branches. The *Akkadian languages comprise the eastern branch; the southern is primarily the Arabic languages; and the northwest branch includes Canaanite, Hebrew, *Ugaritic and Aramaic. The Semites, not so much a cultural unity as a linguistic one, gave to civilization the alphabet and the *Decalogue, among other accomplishments.

Semitism. A word or grammatical construction characteristic of Semitic languages (e.g., Hebrew and Aramaic). We find Semitisms in the *Septuagint and in the NT because of the intersection of Greek and Semitic cultures during this period. The infancy narratives of Luke (Lk 1—2), for example, are noted for their Semitisms. *See also* Aramaism; Hellenism, hellenization; Semites.

sensus literalis. A Latin term meaning "literal sense." The literal or "plain" sense of a passage may seem obvious to some, but no more vexing problem has confronted interpreters of the Bible. Since the eighteenth century, the literal sense has been reduced to the "original" meaning of a passage in its historical context. This reduction, however, has turned reading the Bible into little more than historical research, into recovering a supposed original situation of a passage. The problem is that recovering such an original situation is largely speculative, since our knowledge of such contexts is always changing and our explanations of those contexts change with even more frequency. The plain sense of any text is dependent upon the context from which the interpreter interprets the text. A context can be linguistic and historical, to be sure, but context can also include literary, cultural and theological factors. For example, a Christian interpreting Isaiah 53 has a different context than a Jew, by virtue of the Christian perspective shaped by the suffering and death of Jesus. The Christian may well see in the words of Isaiah a surplus of meaning that is not evident to someone who does not share faith in the death and resurrection of Jesus. Some recent discussions of the problem, notably by Brevard *Childs, seek to recover a literal sense that takes into consideration the scope, purpose and intent of a passage *as Scripture*, not simply in terms of a supposed original situation. *See also* Biblical Theology Movement; canonical criticism; *peshat*; *sensus plenior*.

sensus plenior. A Latin term meaning "the fuller sense." This is the additional or deeper sense of a passage that the author may not have intended but, in the light of other biblical texts (especially NT texts and christological interpretations) or doctrines is "intended" (by God). *Sensus plenior* arose as a concept in the early part of the twentieth century, mostly among Roman Catholic theologians, as an endeavor to articulate new classifications for the senses of Scripture. The *sensus literalis* (literal sense) had been reduced to its grammatical and historical reference, and a new classification was needed to refer to the truth of interpretations that were "more than" the surface meaning of a passage. *Sensus plenior* is the attempt to give weight to interpretations that gain significance in the light of later revelation or the teachings of the church.

Septuagint. The Greek translation of the *Hebrew Bible. This Greek translation was undertaken by the Greek-speaking Jews in Alexandria from the third to the second century B.C. The tradition recounted in the *Letter of *Aristeas* was that seventy-two Jewish scholars (*Septuagint* comes from the Latin term for "seventy," and the abbreviation *LXX is the Roman numeral for seventy) completed the translation in seventy-two days, working separately and by invitation of Ptolemy II Philadelphus (285-246 B.C.). The Septuagint is paramount for biblical scholars both as a witness to the Hebrew text at that time and for an understanding of how certain words and texts were understood during the *Second Temple period. *See also* textual criticism.

Septuagintism. Words and phrases having characteristics of the Greek OT (*LXX) and used by writers of the NT, such as Luke in Acts 2:14, 15-39 and 3:12-26.

Servant Songs. Texts found in Isaiah 40—55 that speak of the "Servant of the Lord" who will suffer for the redemption of Israel. In Jewish tradition, the Servant is generally identified as Israel itself rather than an individual. In Christian tradition, the Servant is one of the key images Jesus uses to speak of his messianic mission. For example, Jesus says, "For the Son of Man came not to be served but to serve, and to give his life as a ransom for many" (Mk 10:45; cf. Is 53:10-12).

Shammai. A leading rabbinical teacher at the turn of the first century (c. 50 B.C.-A.D. 30). Shammai interpreted and applied the Jewish law more rigidly than his counterpart, *Hillel. His views generally prevailed before the destruction of the temple in A.D. 70. His followers are identified as the "house" or "school" of Shammai.

shekinah. The glory or presence of God, especially in his holy dwelling in Jerusalem. The word *šᵉkînâ* is a Hebrew but not a biblical term. It was used by the rabbis to emphasize the relationship between God and Israel.

Shema. Literally, "Hear!"; the opening word and thus the title of a daily Jewish prayer. The words of the prayer are found in Deuteronomy 6:4: "Hear, O Israel, the LORD is our God, the Lord alone." The Shema is not only a prayer but a creed of Jewish belief, that God is one, that one is to observe the commandments, and that God will reward those who observe his *Torah and punish those who do not observe it. These words are often the first words that Jewish children learn. Many Jewish martyrs recited these as their final words.

Shemoneh Esreh. "The Eighteen Benedictions," or daily prayers, used by Jewish worshipers as early as the first century A.D., probably in the synagogues.

Sheol. Abode of the dead. Sheol is the most common OT word to refer to the abode of the dead. The term is not known in the literature of the surrounding cultures. In the OT a person who dies descends to "the pit" (Is 14:15) and the place of "shades" (Job 26:5). All are equal in Sheol (Job 3:11-19), and none return (Job 7:9). In Sheol the dead do not praise God (Ps 6:5). Death, the grave, Sheol, judgment and life beyond death are realities in the Bible but are not developed in much detail, though the NT says more about the afterlife in the light of Jesus' resurrection. Yet even in the NT, the comments are brief and suggestive, not fully developed (as they are even in some extrabiblical Jewish literature).

Sitz im Leben. German term translated "setting in life" or "life situation." *Sitz im Leben* is a technical term used especially by *form critics to refer to the social setting within the life of Israel, Jesus or the early church that enabled individual parables, legends, prophecies, ethical teachings, liturgical formulas, and the like to take shape. With reference to Jesus, for example, one might ask, "What was the *Sitz im Leben* of the early church that led to the recollection, proclamation and application of this saying of Jesus?"

socioscientific interpretation. The application of sociological, anthropological, political and sociocultural theories to biblical texts in order to better understand the nature of Israel or early Christianity. This approach has become popular in current studies of ancient Israel, Jesus, Paul and the early church. Various topics have been fruitfully explored, such as male and female relationships, family and household structures, codes of purity, honor and shame, and patron-client relationships.

sopherim. Scribes or scholars (Heb $s\bar{o}p^e r\hat{i}m$, "scribes") of the *Second Temple period. The *sopherim* expounded the *Torah and promulgated the *oral Torah. They functioned as a bridge between the prophets and the Pharisees, though little is known of them until the time of the Pharisees. Ezra is generally seen as the original scribe, and Simon the Just of the Great *Synagogue is seen as the last.

source criticism. An approach to texts that seeks to discover the literary sources of a document. The assumption is that certain biblical texts underwent a lengthy process of growth and composition, both *oral and written. Source critics examine texts in order to discover evidence of sources on the basis of language and style, the use of divine names, doublets of stories and any discrepancies within or between passages. In OT studies, the most prominent field for source criticism has been the *Pentateuch. Source critics, for example, observe that Genesis 1—2:4a uses the name Elohim when referring to God, and is an orderly and tightly constructed account of creation, with the humans male and female, being the climax of creation. In contrast, Genesis 2 uses Yahweh Elohim, is a story (not a day-by-day account and has Adam being created first, then Eve. Thus source critics conclude that these two different accounts of creation derived from two different sources, the *Priestly source (P) and the *Yahwist source (J) respectively. In the study of the Gospels, source critics have the four Gospels, and particularly the three *Synoptic Gospels, to compare with each other in order to construct the literary sources used. Source criticism addresses the problem of disparity between styles and accounts in a single document, but does not answer the question of how these accounts now fit into a unified composition. *See also* Documentary Hypothesis; Four-Source Hypothesis; Two-Source Hypothesis.

stela. A stone pillar commemorating an event. The pillar would be carved and inscribed with a celebratory description of the event commemorated, usually a military victory. *See also* Merneptah Stela; Moabite Stone.

Strauss, David Friedrich (1808-1874). Controversial German scholar. Strauss's brilliant and provocative book, *Life of Jesus Critically Examined* (2 vols., 1835-1836), was particularly controversial for its designation of anything supernatural in the *Gospels—such as miracles, angels and demons—as *mythological. The unpopularity of his proposals led to his being transferred from the Protestant seminary at the University of Tübingen to the department of classics, then to the University of Zurich, and finally his abandonment of theology. *See also* *Bultmann, Rudolf.

structuralism. A method of study that shares features with literary studies but broadens its scope to include not only the story but also linguistic and cultural elements. The structures of interest to structuralism are grouped into sets and schematized into polar opposites (or "binary opposites," also called "deep structures") that are rooted in universal human experience (good/bad; man/woman; life/death). Instead of trying to find meaning inherent in the words or thoughts themselves, structuralists examine the ways humans shape their thoughts and expressions. The methodology comes from the social anthropology of Claude Lévi-Strauss and was applied to other literature by A. J. Greimas and to biblical literature by Roland Barthes.

Succession Narrative. The account of the transfer of kingship from David to Solomon. The shift from a theocratic *tribal confederacy (in which God rules) to rule by a king brought about many social, political and religious changes in the life of God's people. The rather candid portrait of David and these changing events are recorded in 2 Samuel 9—20, 1 Kings 1—2, with reminders in 2 Samuel 6—7 that it is the word of God delivered through his prophet Nathan that is the ground of hope for Israel, not the often-erring descendents of David.

Sumer, Sumeria. The lower part of southern *Mesopotamia. It is difficult to distinguish a distinct Sumerian culture, though many scholars have attempted to do so. The region was virtually bilingual from its earliest historical period (third millennium B.C.), with Sumerian, on the one hand, being distinct from *Akkadian, a *Semitic language (though many Sumerian words were taken over into Akkadian). By the middle of the second millennium B.C., Sumerian was being used primarily for literary or religious purposes, and thus it remains an important language today for understanding the forms and *genres of ancient Near Eastern texts as a background to the study of the OT.

suzerainty treaties. A type of treaty between a suzerain, or powerful monarch, and a vassal, or petty king. In the Late Bronze Age (1550-1200 B.C.), the Hittite Empire (located in eastern Turkey) sought to control their neighbors to the south (modern day Syria) by entering into treaties. These treaties or covenants between the *suzerain* and *vassal* formed the basis for a political relationship. Similar treaty forms have been discovered in Neo-Assyrian texts dating to the seventh century B.C. Some scholars posit that the *covenant between Israel and her King, Yahweh, is structured on these suzerain-vassal treaties of unequal partners. Others note the differences between the treaties and the covenant (especially in Exodus): the lack of curses and preponderance of blessings, the fraternal grounds, and the didactic function over legal aspects in the biblical covenants.

synagogue. An assembly or place of assembly for Jews to pray, study and worship. The English term *synagogue* is derived from the Greek word *synagōgē*, meaning either a group of people who assemble, or the place where people assembled (see *ekklēsia)*. In the NT we see the Jewish people using the synagogue as a place of prayer, study and worship (Lk 4:16-30; Acts 13:15; 14:1; 15:21;

17:1-3) as well as a place for administering justice (Mk 13:9; Jn 9:22; 12:42; 16:2; Acts 22:19; 2 Cor 11:24). The synagogue became a model for early Christian house churches.

Synagogue, the Great. An assembly (Heb *keneset*) of distinguished rabbis who passed on teachings of the *Torah. The Great Synagogue is mentioned in the Mishnah (*m. ʾAbot* 1:1-2) and in the Talmud. Tradition states that it consisted of either 85 or 120 men, and that it began with Ezra in the sixth century B.C. (cf. Neh 8—9) and ended with Simon the Just, around 200 B.C. Critical scholarship has questioned whether the Great Synagogue ever existed. *See also sopherim.*

syncretism. A blending of varied and often contradictory tenets and practices from various religions into one system, or simply adapting and assimilating foreign ideas and practices into one religion (Gk *syn* + *krasis*, "mixing, blending"). Both Judaism and Christianity were susceptible to syncretism and were repeatedly warned by their leaders (prophets, apostles, etc.) to maintain orthodoxy in doctrine and purity in ethics.

synopsis (of the Gospels). A book that organizes the parallel material in the *Synoptic Gospels (Matthew, Mark, Luke), and sometimes the Gospel of John, in vertical columns so that readers can quickly observe the differences and similarities between them. The term comes from the Greek *syn* ("together") and *optikos* ("see"), thus a "seeing together" or "to view at the same time." An example is Kurt Aland, *Synopsis of the Four Gospels* (United Bible Society, 1985).

Synoptic Gospels. The *Gospels of Matthew, Mark and Luke. These three Gospels are notable for their similarities (they use much of the same material), and thus they "see together" the story of Jesus. *See also* Griesbach, Johann Jakob; synopsis (of the Gospels); Synoptic Problem.

Synoptic Problem. The "problem" of how to account for the similarities and differences that exist among the three *Synoptic Gospels. The term is attributed to J. J. *Griesbach (1745-1812). Most scholars today believe the Mark was the first *Gospel to be written and that Matthew and Luke used Mark as a source, along with a sayings source identified as *Q. *See also* Two-Source Hypothesis.

T

Table of Nations. The listing of the nations in Genesis 10. These nations are described as the descendents of Noah who fulfill the blessing of the Lord to "be fruitful and multiply, and fill the earth" (Gen 9:1). The Table of Nations takes the form of a segmented genealogy, in which the descendents branch out, rather than a vertical genealogy, in which son follows father through several generations (usually tied to a promise of God, e.g., Abraham, Isaac and Jacob). The Table of Nations also accounts for the diversification of peoples (and may, therefore, be *etiological in nature) throughout the Mediterranean world and beyond.

Talmud. A definitive compendium of *rabbinic law setting forth the beliefs and practices of Judaism. In Jewish tradition, when God gave the *Torah to Moses on Mount Sinai, he gave it in two forms: the written Torah and the *oral Torah. The written Torah consists of the first five books of the Bible, the *Pentateuch. The oral Torah refers to further discussions and rulings on points of law as changing circumstances dictated, and these were passed down as oral tradition from generation to generation. The *Mishnah ("study"), written in Hebrew, was codified in the second century A.D.; the Gemarah ("completion"), a commentary on the Mishnah, was written in Aramaic and codified in two forms, the Babylonian and the Jerusalem, during the sixth century A.D. Together the Mishnah and the Gemarah form the Talmud(s). The Torah and the Talmud form the basis for orthodox Jewish faith and practice.

Tanak. An acronym (also Tanach) for the Hebrew Scriptures: *Torah (Law), *Nebiim (Prophets), *Ketubim (Writings). As early as the second century B.C. we find references to the Torah (or "Moses") and the Prophets as authoritative writings (see *canon), but the final section, the Writings, remained amorphous at least until the end of the first century A.D. Luke 24:44 refers to the "law of Moses, the prophets, and the psalms" as a threefold division. In 2 Esdras 14:45-46 we have twenty-four books referred to, while Jerome counts twenty-two, the same number of letters as the Hebrew alphabet (different numberings can occur pending on which books are combined; e.g., Ezra and Nehemiah viewed as a single book). The order can also be fluid, es

in the Writings, where we find either Chronicles or Psalms closing out the section. The *Masoretic order commonly follows this
pattern: Torah (Genesis—Deuteronomy); Nebiim (Former
Prophets: Joshua—Kings, but not Ruth; and Latter Prophets: Isaiah, Jeremiah, Ezekiel and the Twelve [the Minor Prophets], but
not Daniel or Lamentations); and Ketubim (the remaining books,
including Daniel, Lamentations, and Ruth, with Chronicles concluding).

Tannaim. Rabbinic teachers, from the Aramaic term for "study" or
"repeat." The term designates the rabbis whose activity spans
roughly A.D. 20-200. Their predecessors were the great rabbis *Hillel and *Shammai. The Tannaim were responsible for first setting
down into writing the *Mishnah and other *midrashic texts. *See also* rabbinic Judaism; Talmud.

Targum. Oral and written Aramaic translation and interpretation of
the *Hebrew Bible (from the Heb word meaning "paraphrase"; pl.
Targumim). When the Jews returned from *Babylonian exile, Aramaic emerged as the common language of the people. Thus when
Scripture was read in the *synagogues, the reader ($m^e t \hat{u} r g^e m \bar{a} n$, "interpreter") provided paraphrases in Aramaic. These paraphrases
were passed on and eventually written down beginning in the
third century A.D. By the fifth century, two Targums had become
standard: *Targum Onqelos* on the *Torah, and *Targum Jonathan* on
the Prophets. The Targums are important witnesses to the biblical
text in this early period of transmission, but because of their freedom to expound the text, they are equally important for how the
text was interpreted by the Jewish community. *See also* textual criticism.

Tatian. *See Diatessaron.*

Teaching of the Twelve Apostles, The. *See Didache, the.*

Ten Commandments. *See* Decalogue.

tendency criticism. A methodology that attempts to discern the tendencies of NT documents. The method is associated with F. C.
*Baur (and the *Tübingen School), who analyzed the origin, date
and character of the NT writings for the author's *Tendenz* ("tendency, aim, or bias"). Luke's *Tendenz* in Acts, for example, was to
create an irenic picture of the church by minimizing the differences between Peter and Paul. *See also* redaction criticism.

terminus a quo. A Latin term used in chronological discussion to designate the "earliest" time (literally, "boundary from which") an event could have taken place or a document could have been written.

terminus ad quem. A Latin term used in chronological discussion to designate the "latest" time (literally, "boundary to which") an event could have taken place or a document could have been written. For example, 5/4 B.C. and A.D. 33/34 mark the *terminus a quo and the *terminus ad quem* respectively of the life of Jesus.

Tertullian (c. 155/160-225/250). The first church father (from Carthage, North Africa) to write in Latin. He is known for his apologetic (*Apologia*), theological (*De baptismo*) and ascetic writings. His *Adversus Marcionem (Against Marcion)* shows his active opposition to the heretic *Marcion. In biblical studies, Tertullian affirmed the unity of the Jewish and Christian Scriptures and the rule of faith (*regula fides*) of the apostolic church.

Testaments of the Twelve Patriarchs. A *pseudepigraphical document (c. 109-106 B.C.), probably inspired by and modeled on Jacob's farewell to his twelve sons (Gen 49) and Moses' final blessing on Israel (Deut 33). The books contain moral encouragement, spiritual consolation and predictions of the divine blessings and punishments that await God's people in the future messianic age. The work has considerable historical and theological value for NT studies. *See also* farewell discourse.

testimonia. A hypothetical collection of OT texts used by early Christians for apologetic or preaching purposes. The possibility of early Christian *testimonia* is based on the NT writers' use of certain Scriptures to supplement their theological and apologetic arguments or to support certain Christian beliefs about the person and purpose of Jesus as a fulfillment of the OT. Such *testimonia* may have circulated in oral form as part of early Christian preaching and teaching before they were incorporated into an author's work. The only extant collection of such Scriptures comes from the *Dead Sea Scrolls: 4QTestimonia is a series of OT quotations demonstrating the messianic expectations of the *Qumran community. Matthew makes extensive use of OT citations, which suggests does not prove—the possibility of an independent collection he could reference. Paul used a collection of OT prooftex various sources: Psalms and Isaiah in his discussion of righteous-ness in Romans 3:10-20; Hosea, Isaiah and others when he discuss-es the Gentiles (see Rom 9:24-33; 15:9-12). Romans 1:17 and Galatians 3:11 use Habakkuk 2:4 to show that justification is by faith. Finally, 1 Peter 2:6-8 joins Isaiah 8:14 and 28:16 when speak-ing of salvation.

Tetragrammaton. The four-letter name for God in Judaism (Gk *tetragrammaton*, "four-letter word"). In Jewish tradition the holy name of God is not pronounced, and the "four letters" are written without vowels as YHWH. In Jewish texts today the name of God is often represented either by "G-d" or *HaShem*, "the Name," rather than by the four letters and is frequently pronounced as *Adonai*, "Lord." *See also* Yahweh, YHWH.

Tetrateuch. The first four books of the *Hebrew Bible viewed as an integral unit. Rather than dividing the *Torah into a *Pentateuch ("five books"), some scholars suggest that the first four *(tetra)* books belong together and that Deuteronomy—2 Kings (the *Deu-teronomistic History) form another integral unit. However, the theological significance of the *Pentateuch should not be over-looked in literary and historical considerations.

textual criticism. The scholarly discipline of establishing the text as near to the original as possible or probable (also known as *lower criticism). Since we no longer have any original manu-scripts, or "autographs," scholars must sort and evaluate the ex-tant copies with their variant wordings. For example, errors commonly occur when letters are confused (in Hebrew the *dālet* [ד]and the *rêš* [ר]are easily confused), when letters and words are omitted (*haplography; *homoioteleuton) or written more than once (*dittography), and when letters are transposed (*met-athesis) or juxtaposed from parallel words or texts. The textual critic not only sorts through manuscripts and fragments for copyist errors but also considers early translations (such as the *Vulgate or *Peshitta) and *lectionaries for their witness to the ∍xt. For example, the *Septuagint sometimes has a reading that ฺears older or closer to what scholars think was the original ⸱ of the *Hebrew Bible and can form the basis of an emenda-ʹa correction of a text that seems to have been corrupted in ꓪission). It is not always clear, however, when an ancient translation is preserving a different text or rendering a word or verse in a more comprehensible way. Textual criticism is often seen as the most objective of the various biblical criticisms because there are clear rules governing the establishment of texts. However, judgments regarding any textual reading involve an element of interpretation, so disagreements remain. *See also* Dead Sea Scrolls; Targum.

Textus Receptus. Latin for "received text." In OT studies this term is occasionally used loosely for the Second Rabbinic Bible of Jacob ben Chayyim, published in the sixteenth century. This text also contains the *Targum, or Aramaic translation, of the *Hebrew Bible, and the most important Jewish commentaries (*Rashi, Kimchi, *Ibn Ezra, etc.). More recent critical editions have opted for the Ben Asher text (Codex Leningradensis) as less eclectic and more reliable (the principles upon which the Ben Asher text is based are more consistent than the Ben Chayyim text). The term is most often used in NT studies to refer to *Erasmus's Greek text of 1535. The Authorized, or King James, Version of the Bible is based upon the Textus Receptus. The Textus Receptus is widely criticized today because of the haste with which it was produced and its heavy reliance on late rather than early Greek manuscripts. *See also* textual criticism.

thanksgiving psalms. *See* hymn.

theios anēr. *See* aretalogy; divine man.

Theodore of Mopsuestia (c. 350-428). Early church father. So great was Theodore's influence in the Eastern Church that later commentators gave him the title "the Blessed Exegete." Born to wealthy parents in Antioch, he, with John *Chrysostom, was educated by the eminent philosopher Libanius. Theodore left his secular career for a monastic life. A prominent member of the *Antiochene school, Theodore's exegesis is marked by his knowledge of Hebrew (though he relied almost exclusively on the *Septuagint translation), his familiarity with the historical circumstances of the Hebrews and his clear understanding of biblical idiom (because, in part, of his training in rhetoric). He wr a treatise, now lost, *Against the Allegorists.*

theologia crucis. A term (literally, "theology of the cross") us Martin Luther to emphasize God's divine self-revelation suffering and the cross of Christ.

theologoumenon. From the Greek and Latin meaning "to speak of God." The term usually refers to the historicization of theological statements derived from speculation on divine things and logical inferences from revelation rather than based on historical evidence. For example, the genealogy of Jesus and his virgin birth are classified by some as theologoumena derived from beliefs that Jesus was the son of David and the Son of God.

theophany. Literally, a "manifestation of God." Theophanies in the Bible usually are accompanied by physical signs: earth shaking or quaking, a cloud, fire or other visible means of display. For example, when God appears to Moses in a burning bush (Ex 3) or when the prophet Micah announces that God is coming and that the mountains will melt and the valleys will burst open (1:4). A theophany shows God's power and involvement in the world, as well as his favor (or disfavor) with events or people.

Therapeutae. A mysterious group of Jewish healers and miracle workers (from the Gk *therapeuō*, "to heal") mentioned by *Philo. Usually, but not unanimously, they are classified as a branch of the *Essenes because of their apparently similar beliefs and practices, such as asceticism, celibacy and communal living.

Third Isaiah. Chapters 56—66 of Isaiah, believed by many scholars to have been written by a different author than *Second Isaiah (40—55) or First Isaiah (1—39). It is also call Trito-Isaiah. The style is distinctive at points, and the themes and setting of these chapters have suggested a postexilic setting in the land of Palestine. *See also* Babylonian exile; Isaiah, multiple authorship of.

Thomas Aquinas. *See* Aquinas, Thomas (1225-1274).

toledoth **formula.** The formula "These are the generations/descendents [Heb *tôlᵉdôt*] of," which is repeated in Genesis as a structural device. The formula reinforces the major theme of the beginnings and continuity of the human race. The first appearance of the formula occurs in Genesis 2:4 and serves to link the creation of the cosmos (Gen 1) with the history of humanity (Gen 2—3); throughout the text it marks junctures and developments in the story.

topos. A commonplace theme taken up in oratory or literary forms, including letters. In the NT we encounter topoi (pl. of topos) as expanded *paraenetical statements (or miniature essays) on specific themes or topics. A topos is distinguished from loosely strung ethical admonitions by its distinctive rhetorical structure, which often follows the pattern of injunction, rationale, discussion and possibly analogy. Examples include Paul's discussion of the state (Rom 13:1-7), eating certain foods (Rom 14:1-23), Christian life in light of the coming eschaton (1 Thess 5:1-11), James's discussion on partiality (Jas 2:1-13) and the tongue (Jas 3:1-12), and Peter's guide for holy living (1 Pet 1:13-16).

Torah. The first part of the Hebrew *canon, corresponding to the *Pentateuch. It is traditionally translated "law" based upon the Greek translation of Hebrew *tôrâ* in the *Septuagint, *nomos*. More recent attempts at translation use "instruction" as a way to avoid the theological and judicial associations of law, and to acknowledge that *tôrâ* is more than law in the narrow, legal sense. The Torah encompasses all that the first five books of the Bible contain—saga, laws, songs, genealogies, and so forth. The term can also be used of the OT as a whole, including even the *Talmud, so it comes to have the sense of God's revelation as a whole and not just commands or laws. Instructive are passages such as Psalm 1:2, where the righteous "delight" in Torah, and Psalms 19 and 119, which are extended poems on the worth of Torah. Torah sets forth the fundamentals of Israelite faith and functions as the norm for judging all subsequent experiences of God. *See also* Pentateuch; Tanak.

Tosefta. Aramaic term meaning "additions" (often written in the plural, *Tosafot*). These are a series of commentaries on the *Mishnah written by rabbis from the second to fourth centuries A.D.

tradent. A person or group of persons who preserve and re-present a tradition or traditions. Michael Fishbane makes the helpful distinction between *traditum*, the content of the tradition, and *traditio*, the manner in which the tradition is transmitted (*Biblical Interpretation in Ancient Israel*, 1985). Tradents do not simply reproduce the tradition but reactualize it in new and fresh ways. Chronicles is an obvious example of reworking traditional sources (especially 1 and 2 Samuel, 1 and 2 Kings), and many scholars argue that Matthew and Luke had Mark as their primary source. We can also see this process in legal material: Deuteronomy 5:12-15 gives the exodus event as the motivation for keeping the sabbath, while Exodus 20:8-11 makes reference to creation.

tradition criticism. An approach to a text that seeks to explain the ways various historical traditions developed over the course of their *oral tradition. For example, stories that circulated in different circles of the *patriarchs might eventually have been brought together and linked into a larger unit, or oracles that a prophet spoke during the Assyrian crisis might have been expanded for use during the Babylonian crisis. Jesus' teachings and stories likewise passed through various stages of oral tradition before they were given their final form. The tradition critic attempts to trace these traditions through their various stages to their final redaction or compilation. *See also* form criticism; Jesus tradition; redaction criticism.

Traditionsgeschichte. A German term translated "tradition history." *See* also tradition criticism.

transfiguration. An event recorded in all three *Synoptic Gospels (Mt 17:1-8; Mk 9:2-8; Lk 9:28-36; cf. 2 Pet 1:16-18) in which Jesus' appearance underwent a metamorphosis (Gk *metamorphoō,* "to be changed in form, transformed"). In the *Gospel accounts of the transfiguration, Elijah and Moses conversed with Jesus, his clothing became dazzling white, and God's voice was heard from a cloud saying, "This is my Son, the Beloved; with him I am well pleased; listen to him!" (Mt 17:5). This incident was a preview of Jesus' glory after the resurrection.

Trent, Council of. *See* Council of Trent.

tribal confederacy. *See* amphictyony.

triple tradition. Material that is common to the three *Synoptic Gospels. This terms avoids alluding to the sources as in the *Two- or *Four-Source theories.

Trito-Isaiah. *See* Third Isaiah.

Tübingen School. The followers of F. C. *Baur, centered around the University of Tübingen, who adopted his interpretation of early Christianity and his principles of biblical interpretation. Although widely criticized for its historical skepticism and radical presuppositions, "the ghost of Baur" continues to survive in some circles.

gendkatalog. See catalogue of vices and virtues.

o-Source Hypothesis. A theory that attempts to explain the composition of the *Synoptic Gospels by positing that Matthew and e used materials from two distinct sources (Mark and *Q). The theory is grounded in the fact that Matthew reproduces approximately 90 percent of Mark, Luke reproduces approximately 57 percent of Mark, and there are approximately 230 verses in Matthew and Luke that may be attributable to the Q source.

two-ways tradition. A motif in ancient and Christian moral instruction that develops the metaphor of two ways or paths of life. Humanity has a choice of living either a virtuous life or a life of vice; of manifesting the works of the flesh or the fruit of the Spirit; of living in truth or perversity, in light or in darkness. This motif is evident in the OT, in *Qumran literature and especially in the *paraenetic sections of the NT (e.g., Gal 5:13-26; Eph 4:17—5:20; Jas 4:1-10; 1 Pet 4:1-6; 2 Pet 2:1-2). The *Didache also has a lengthy section on the "way of life" and the "way of death" (*Did*.1.1—6.2). *See also* wisdom psalms.

type scene. A scene in a story that serves as a literary convention for other scenes. Parallel or repetitious scenes, such as a bitter rivalry between a barren wife and a fertile wife or concubine (Sarah and Hagar; Hannah and Peninnah), can be seen as part of the *oral tradition of stories, as different sources (according to *source criticism) or as literary conventions, that is, as a part of the literary artistry of biblical narratives. With a type scene, an author can draw upon the expectations of the audience and remake those expectations by varying the conventions. Every culture has literary conventions that it uses with variations. "Once upon a time" and "In a galaxy far, far away" are modern examples of such conventions. *See also Leitmotiv; Leitwort.*

typology. Biblical comparisons and links made between persons, events, things and institutions of one biblical period and those of another, particularly between those of the OT and the NT. The term is derived from the Greek word *typos,* meaning "impression, mark, image" and, by metaphorical extension, an example or model. Typology is employed by the biblical authors to show continuity in God's plan, the "pattern in the carpet" of redemptive history. Typological interpretation is the attempt to detect types in the biblical text, and like *allegorical interpretation, it suffers from the excesses of some of its practitioners. The *type* is the initial person, event, thing or institution; the corresponding and later person, event, thing or institution is called the *antitype.* For example portrays Christ as the antitype of Adam in Romans 5:12-21: "Adam, who is a *type* of the one who was to come" (Rom 5:14). Typology should be distinguished from *intertextuality, though some overlap is natural. Types are not essentially chronological and certainly not causal or in opposition. Rather, typology works on the assumption of the oneness of the divine plan in which all events and persons are parts and reflections of that plan. Thus the "horizontal" element (along the historical plane) is not as important as the "vertical" element, where the facts of the events are seen in the larger structure of divine reality. Furthermore, Christian typological interpretation has its fulfillment in the person and work of Jesus Christ; it is not simply the correspondences that occupy our interpretation but the fulfillment of those correspondences in the life, death and resurrection of Jesus. Rather than an artificial correspondence between every OT person and institution and Jesus Christ—and the virtual reduction of these persons and institutions into mere shades—a truly theological typology sees the events and persons transfigured and completed in Jesus. Thus, the sacrifice of Isaac, Abraham's "beloved son," in Genesis 22 is picked up in the NT as a type of Christ, God's beloved Son given for all. God's redemptive activity in the one event comes to completion in the second. Both occurrences are real and concrete, but they transcend mere chronological or causal correspondence and signify the ongoing redemptive activity of God in creation.

U

Ugarit, Ugaritic. A city-state situated on the north coast of Syria (modern-day Ras Shamra) during the Late Bronze Age (1550-1200 B.C.), and the Northwest Semitic language of that culture. The discovery of the Ras Shamra Texts at Ugarit has given scholars the most direct and thorough evidence of Canaanite language, literature and religion during the time of the ancient Israelites, and since Ugaritic is quite similar to ancient Hebrew and other Canaanite languages, it provides valuable information about the meanings of obscure OT words and the cultural and religious practices of Israel's neighbors. As with all comparative studies, caution must be used in what kinds of conclusions can be drawn; both similarities and differences must be balanced in the final assessment.

uncial. The uppercase or square-type letters, also called majuscules, that were characteristic of Greek manuscripts written on *parchment (vellum) from the third to the ninth or tenth centuries A.D.

Urevangelium. A primitive, or original, *Gospel (German *Ur*, "early, original, primitive," + *evangelium*, "Gospel"). The term represents an attempt by some German scholars to explain the *Synoptic Problem by proposing that an early Hebrew or Aramaic *Gospel was used as a source by Matthew, Mark and Luke to write their Gospels. Similarities and differences in the Synoptics are sometimes explained in terms of different Greek *recensions of this *Ur* Gospel. *See also* Four-Source Hypothesis; Two-Source Hypothesis.

Urgemeinde. A German term often retained in English-language studies when discussing the early church (*Ur*, "early," + *Gemeinde*, "congregation, community") because the word captures the essence of the early church better that the word *Kirche* ("church").

Urmarkus. A primitive version of Mark's *Gospel (German *Ur*, "early," + *Markus*, "Mark"). This name was first given by H. J. Holtzmann in 1863 to a hypothetical literary source (*Urform*) that he believed Mark used to write his Gospel (and was lacking those Markan passages that Matthew and Luke omit). This hypothesis has not found support among scholars, and there is no evidence that such a document existed. Most scholars claim that Mark's Gospel is based mainly on *oral traditions about Jesus that may, for example, have come from apostles, particularly Peter. *See also Urevangelium.*

V

vaticinium ex eventu. A Latin phrase (pl. *vaticinia ex eventu*) literally translated "prophesying from an outcome." In other words, a *vaticinium ex eventu* would not be a true prediction but a prophecy placed in the mouth of a narrative figure in light of an event (o events) that actually did transpire. In the *Gospels, for examp' some interpreters have claimed that *vaticinia ex eventu* occu' Jesus' sayings, such as his prediction of the destruction of the ple (Mt 24:2; Mk 13:2; Lk 19:43-44; 21:6, 22; cf. also Mk 10: 14:28, Lk 19:42). Amos 5:1-3 laments the fall of Jerusalem a' complished fact even though it has not yet happened during Amos's lifetime.

vellum. *See* parchment.

version. In textual studies, it denotes the translation of the Bible from Hebrew and Greek into other languages such as Latin, Syriac and Ethiopic.

vice and virtue catalogue. *See* catalogue of vices and virtues.

Vorlage. A literary source or prototype (German, "that which lies before") that lies behind an extant composition of a biblical text. In Gospel studies, for example, Luke and Matthew may have used an early copy (*Vorlage*) of Mark that differed in some ways from the *canonical Mark that we currently possess. In Old Testament studies, J, E, D and P (*see* Documentary Hypothesis) are seen by some as the *Vorlagen* (sources) of the Pentateuch. The *Vorlage* of 1 and 2 Chronicles is 1 and 2 Samuel and 1 and 2 Kings. *See also* Urevangelium; Urmarkus.

Vulgate. The Latin translation of the Bible by *Jerome in the fourth century A.D. (Latin *vulgo*, "to make common, accessible"). It is characterized by its adherence to the *hebraica veritas* (the Hebrew text of the OT) rather than reliance on the *Septuagint or other Greek translations. It thus becomes another witness to the state of the Hebrew Old Testament and Greek New Testament in the centuries following the NT period. *See also* textual criticism.

W

Wellhausen, Julius (1844-1918). German OT scholar. Wellhausen transformed the face of OT studies with his work on the dating of the sources in the *Pentateuch. The *Documentary Hypothesis did not originate with him, but he combined literary analysis with a *history of religions approach that captured the imagination of scholars and defined the debate ever since. For Wellhausen, the prophets were the true innovators of Israelite religion with their notion of "ethical monotheism." The Pentateuch's *cul-'c laws came much later in the development of Israelite religion, ʌrking a move to a legalism that was not part of the original ssage.

ʌschauung. German term for "worldview, philosophy of life, ʾgy." The term is occasionally used in biblical studies to designate the totality of a text's cultural, philosophical and theological perspective.

Westcott, Brooke Foss (1825-1901). British NT scholar and textual critic. Westcott and F. J. A. *Hort are best known for their significant insights and contributions to the science of NT *textual criticism. The Westcott-Hort edition of the Greek NT (*The New Testament in the Original Greek, With Introduction and Appendix,* 1881) took twenty-eight years to complete. In it the authors identify four major text types (Syrian, Western, Alexandrian, Neutral) and set forth their principles of textual criticism. Westcott, Hort and *Lightfoot formed the Cambridge Trio because of their similar commitment to the text-critical, linguistic and exegetical study of Scripture.

Western text. In NT *textual criticism, the name given by B. F. *Westcott and F. J. A. *Hort to a family of manuscripts with similar textual characteristics that had a Western *provenance (e.g., some Greco-Latin manuscripts, Old Latin, and quotations from the Latin fathers). It is known for its modifications of other textual traditions, especially its additions to the book of Acts.

Wie es eigentlich geschehen ist. A German phrase translated "as it actually happened." It is sometimes quoted as a catch phrase to characterize the assumption prevalent among nineteenth- and twentieth-century historians that past history can be reconstructed just as it originally was.

wisdom christology. The identification of Jesus with God's divine Wisdom as personified in certain OT and Jewish texts (e.g., Job 28; Prov 1:20-23; 8:1-36; Wis 7:7—9:18; Sir 24). Matthew appears to be the first *Gospel writer to identify Jesus this way (11:16-19, 25-27; 12:42; 23:34-39). John presents Jesus as the unique Word, or Wisdom of God (Jn 1:1-18). Paul even earlier identifies Christ as God's wisdom for the believer (1 Cor 1:30; Col 1:15-20; cf. Heb 1:1-3).

wisdom literature. Biblical literature characterized by instruction based upon experience, tradition and the "way the world work rather than emphasizing direct divine disclosure as the sourc truth (as with *Torah or the prophets). This body of literature its roots in antiquity and, though linked with Solomon (1 4:29-30), is marked by observations of wise but otherwise o folks (parents, sages). Wisdom literature existed throug ancient Near East long before Israel came on the scene (e.g., Egyptian instructions dating to the middle of the third millennium B.C.). The *genres and *forms of wisdom literature extend from simple *proverbs to essays and reflections on justice and death, as well as fables and debates. Biblical wisdom books are traditionally identified as Proverbs, Job and Ecclesiastes (Song of Songs is also included in some lists), and Sirach and Wisdom of Solomon in the *Apocrypha. We also find strong wisdom influence in the Psalms (e.g., Ps 1) and in many other books (e.g., the Joseph stories in Genesis and the stories of Daniel and his friends, to which some would add the story of Esther). Defining and delimiting wisdom literature is often problematic. Wisdom is open to all, since it seeks to instruct people to live a well-ordered life, a life lived acknowledging God's ways and intentions for his creation. Yet wisdom instructs through the use of "artful words" and hence requires interpretive skill, patience and a desire to probe the riches of this life (Prov 1:2-6). Israel's contribution to this ancient and international literature is the declaration that wisdom has its source in God, the "fear of the LORD" (Prov 1:7). *See also* Amenemope, Instruction of.

wisdom psalms. Poems written for educational purposes, with characteristics of *wisdom literature. Most *form critics recognize that not all the poems in the Psalter come from *cultic settings; some come from the wisdom tradition and are used primarily for *didactic purposes. For example, Psalm 1 does not follow the form of either *lament or *hymn but admonishes its readers to "delight" in the study of *Torah, God's instruction. There is also an emphasis on the doctrine of the *two ways—the paths and outcomes of the just and the wicked.

Wissenschaft. A German term for science, knowledge or intelligence. It is sometimes carried over into English biblical studies to denote the application of the *historical-critical method (regarded as "scientific" in this German sense) to the study of the Scriptures.

e oracle. A form of prophetic speech announcing impending gment. For example, Amos warns Israel, "Alas for you who de- the day of the Lord! . . . It is darkness, not light" (5:18).

, William (1859-1906). German NT scholar. Wrede is noted rily for his book, *The Messianic Secret in the Gospels* (1901).

His studies with Adolf *Harnack and Albrecht Ritschl were influential for his role in developing the *Religionsgeschichtliche Schule* (*history of religions school) at the University of Göttingen. *See also* Messianic Secret, Quest of the Historical Jesus; Schweitzer, Albert.

Writings. The third section of the Hebrew *canon, called the *Ketubim (or Ketuvim) in Hebrew. *See also* Tanak.

Y

Yahweh, YHWH. The *covenant name God reveals to Moses at Mount Sinai (Ex 3:7-15). It testifies to God's special relationship with his people Israel and his commitment to act on their behalf through his saving deeds. The name is regarded as sacred by Jews, who spell it using only the consonants YHWH (the *Tetragrammaton) and substitute the name Adonai, "Lord," rather than utter the actual name. Modern scholars have tried to approximate the original pronunciation with the spelling Yahweh (formerly it was pronounced Jehovah).

Yahwist. According to the *Documentary Hypothesis, the author of the J source (J from the German "*Jahwist") in the *Pentateuch, a source characterized by its preference for the name *Yahweh when referring to God. The Yahwist narrates the story of Israel from the origins of humanity and the proliferation of sin in the early chapters of Genesis, through the call of Abraham, the deliverance by means of Moses, and the culmination of that story with the revelation of Yahweh on Mount Sinai. The J source is thought by some to have been written in the early monarchical period (tenth century B.C.). The Yahwist is seen as a subtle storyteller with a deep and distinct theological touch. In the Yahwist's perspective, humanity is prone to transgress the limits set by Yahweh, but rather than simple punitive measures, Yahweh seeks to keep humanity from destruction. The Yahwist has been regarded by some as the first great theologian in Israel.

YHWH. *See* Yahweh, YHWH.

Yavneh. *See* Jamnia, Council of.

Z

Zadokite Documents/Fragments. See Damascus Document.

Zealots. A Jewish revolutionary movement. The name comes from the Greek *zēlōtēs,* a person full of zeal, displaying fervent devotion to a cause. The Zealots were a Jewish political party whose devotion to theocracy and *Torah led to violent military clashes against the Roman occupation of Palestine. Their provocations against the Romans precipitated the Roman siege and destruction of Jerusalem in A.D. 70.

Zion. The mount in the city of Jerusalem associated with David and the temple. Zion is rich in symbol and theology. On Zion God chooses to make his presence known visibly in the temple, and the construction of the temple reflects the character of creation in Genesis 1. Zion testifies to God's lordship, not only over Israel and the nations, but over the cosmos itself. It is from Zion that God's *Torah instructs the peoples of the earth (Is 2:2-3; Mic 4:1-2). On Zion, sacred time (sabbath) and sacred space (temple) come together (cf. Ps 132:13-14). The Psalms contains songs (or *hymns) of Zion (cf. Ps 46; 48; 76; 84; 122; 132; 147).

Common Abbreviations

Latin Terms and General Abbreviations
ad loc. ad locum, "at the place"
a fortiori "from a stonger (reason/ argument)"
ante "before"
a posteriori "from what comes after"
a priori "from what is before"
argumentum e silentio "argument from silence"
ca. or c. circa, "about"
cf. confer, "compare"
de facto "in reality, fact,"
e.g. *exempli gratia*, "for example"
ergo "therefore"
et al. *et alii*, "and others"
i.e. *id est*, "that is"
ipso facto "by the fact itself"
κτλ καὶ τὰ λοιπάς, "and the rest" = *et cetera*
magnum opus "great work"
passim "throughout, everywhere"
q.v. *quod vide*, "on which see"
regula fidei "rule of faith"
sic "thus"
sine qua non "without which nothing"
v./vv. or vs./vss. verse/verses
vol(s). volume(s)

Periodicals, Reference Works, Ancient Literature and Bible Translations
AB Anchor Bible
ABD Anchor Bible Dictionary
ANET Ancient Near Eastern Texts Relating to the Old Testament
Ant. Josephus, *Antiquities of the Jews*
Apoc. Apocrypha
AV Authorized Version (or King James Version)
BAR Biblical Archaeology Review
BAGD W. Bauer, W. F. Arndt, F. W. Gingrich, F. W. Danker, *Greek-English Lexicon of the New Testament*
BDB F. Brown, S. R. Driver and C. A. Briggs, *Hebrew and English Lexicon of the Old Testament*

BECNT Baker Exegetical Commentary on the New Testament
Bsac Bibliotheca sacra
BJRL Bulletin of the John Rylands University Library of Manchester
BT Babylonian Talmud
CBQ Catholic Biblical Quarterly
CHB Cambridge History of the Bible
COS Context of Scripture
CTJ Calvin Theological Journal
DBI Dictionary of Biblical Imagery
DJG Dictionary of Jesus and the Gospels
DLNTD Dictionary of the Later New Testament and Its Developments
DNTB Dictionary of New Testament Background
DOTP Dictionary of the Old Testament: Pentateuch
DPL Dictionary of Paul and His Letters
DSS Dead Sea Scrolls
EDNT Exegetical Dictionary of the New Testament
EncJud Encyclopaedia Judaica
EvQ Evangelical Quarterly
ExpT Expository Times
HBD Harper's Bible Dictionary
Herm Hermeneia
HNTC Harper's New Testament Commentaries
HTS Harvard Theological Studies
HUCA Hebrew Union College Annual
IB Interpreter's Bible
IBC Interpretation: A Bible Commentary for Teaching and Preaching
IBD Illustrated Bible Dictionary
ICC International Critical Commentary
IDB Interpreter's Dictionary of the Bible
IDBSup Interpreter's Dictionary of the Bible, Supplementary Volume
Int Interpretation
ISBE International Standard Bible Encyclopedia
JBL Journal of Biblical Literature
JNES Journal of Near Eastern Studies
Jos. Josephus
JQR Jewish Quarterly Review
JSNT Journal for the Study of the New Testament

JSNT Sup Journal for the Study of the New Testament Supplement Series

JSOT Journal for the Study of the Old Testament

JSOTSup Journal for the Study of the Old Testament Supplement Series

JSS Journal of Semitic Studies

J.W. Josephus, *Jewish War*

KJV King James Version

LCL Loeb Classical Library

Louw-Nida J. P. Louw and E. A. Nida, *Greek-English Lexicon*

LSJ H. G. Liddell, R. Scott and H. S. Jones, *Greek-English Lexicon*

LXX Septuagint

MS or MSS manuscript or manuscripts

MT Masoretic Text

NA^{27} Nestle-Aland, *Novum Testamentum Graece*, 27th ed.

NASB New American Standard Bible

NBC New Bible Commentary

NBD New Bible Dictionary

NCB New Century Bible

NDBT New Dictionary of Biblical Theology

NEB New English Bible

Neot Neotestamentica

NIB New Interpreter's Bible

NIBC The New International Biblical Commentary

NICNT The New International Commentary on the New Testament

NICOT The New International Commentary on the Old Testament

NIDNTT New International Dictionary of New Testament Theology

NIDOTTE New International Dictionary of Old Testament Theology and Exegesis

NIGTC New International Greek Testament Commentary

NIV New International Version

NJB New Jerusalem Bible

NKJV New King James Version

NovT Novum Testamentum

NovTSup Supplement to *Novum Testamentum*

NRSV New Revised Standard Version

NTS New Testament Studies

OCD The Oxford Classical Dictionary

OTL Old Testament Library

OTP The Old Testament Pseudepigrapha

PEQ Palestine Exploration Quarterly

RevExp Review and Expositor

RevQ Revue de Qumran

RGG Religion in Geschichte und Gegenwart

RSV Revised Standard Version

SacP Sacra Pagina

SBLDS SBL Dissertation Series

SJT Scottish Journal of Theology

SNTSMS Society for New Testament Studies Monograph Series

Str-B H. L. Strack and P. Billerbeck, *Kommentar zum Neuen Testament aus Talmud und Midrasch*

SWJT Southwestern Journal of Theology

TDNT Theological Dictionary of the New Testament

TDOT Theological Dictionary of the Old Testament

TEV Today's English Version (or Good News for Modern Man)

Them Themelios

TJ Trinity Journal

TNTC Tyndale New Testament Commentary

TS Theological Studies

TynBul Tyndale Bulletin

UBSGNT United Bible Societies *Greek New Testament*

VT Vetus Testamentum

VTSup *Vetus Testamentum* Supplements

WBC Word Biblical Commentary

WTJ Westminster Theological Journal

ZAW Zeitschrift für die alttestamentliche Wissenschaft

ZNW Zeitschrift für die neutestamentliche Wissenschaft

ZPEB Zondervan Pictorial Encyclopedia of the Bible